Tiger of Mysore

Tiger of Mysore

THE LEGACY OF TIPU SULTAN

Mack Rafeal

Spectra Enterprise

Contents

Table of Content

Introduction

In the archives of history, certain figures arise as significant images of obstruction and strength, making a permanent imprint on the embroidered artwork of human experience. One such illuminating presence from the eighteenth century who cut his name into the narratives of rebellion is Tipu King, frequently hailed as the "Tiger of Mysore." His heritage, an intricate exchange of military ability, political insight, and social support, rises above the bounds of time and resounds through the passageways of history.

Tipu Ruler climbed to the lofty position of the Realm of Mysore in 1782, following the downfall of his dad, King Hyder Ali. The Sultanate of Mysore, arranged in the core of the Indian subcontinent, gave testimony regarding Tipu's fleeting ascent and persevering through heritage. As the head of a realm decisively situated in the Deccan locale, Tipu Ruler ended up entrapped in the trap of international relations that described the eighteenth 100 years.

The international scene of the time was set apart by the attack of European powers into the Indian subcontinent, each competing for matchless quality and financial predominance. The English East India Organization, specifically, tried to extend its impact, igniting a progression of struggles that would characterize Tipu King's rule. His experiences with the English were not simple encounters; they were fights that would shape the fate of the area and make a permanent imprint on the pages of history.

Tipu King's sobriquet, the "Tiger of Mysore," embodies the furious and unstoppable soul with which he went up against the difficulties of his time. His tactical missions, set apart by creative systems and an immovable obligation to protecting his realm, procured him a standing as an imposing foe. The Old English Mysore Wars, a progression of struggles battled between the English East India Organization and the Sultanate of Mysore, stand as a demonstration of Tipu King's tactical ability.

Past the war zone, Tipu King's standard was described by a visionary way to deal with administration. He carried out moderate regulatory changes, cultivating monetary turn of events and mechanical development inside his realm. Tipu was a supporter of human expression and sciences, developing a social renaissance that left a permanent engraving on the social texture of Mysore.

Be that as it may, Tipu Ruler's heritage isn't without contention. His steadfast opposition against English expansionism has been hailed as a courageous battle for freedom, however it likewise welcomed the fury of his enemies. The situation that developed during his rule have been dependent upon verifiable understanding and discussion, with viewpoints fluctuating in light of social, public, and philosophical focal points.

The Tiger of Mysore's commitment with the English East India Organization arrived at a basic point with the marking of the Settlement of Mangalore in 1784. The settlement carried an impermanent discontinuance to threats, yet the ghost of contention posed a potential threat not too far off. Ensuing years saw a sensitive dance among strategy and military moving, as Tipu King looked to defend the power of his domain against the infringing English powers.

The scene of Tipu King's standard was not restricted to the domain of political and military undertakings. His obligation to social and strict variety is clear in his support of different networks, encouraging a climate where Hindu, Muslim, and Christian subjects coincided. This inclusivity reached out to his organization, where authorities from various strict foundations served in key positions, adding to a cosmopolitan ethos inside the Sultanate.

The Tiger of Mysore was a tactical strategist and legislator as well as a visionary chief who perceived the significance of mechanical headways in the impacting scene. His endeavors to modernize the military, presenting developments like the utilization of rockets in fighting, exhibited a ground breaking approach that rose above the limits of his period.

In spite of his tactical keenness and moderate strategies, Tipu Ruler's standard confronted its portion of difficulties. The elements of force in the eighteenth century were perplexing, with moving coalitions and international contentions characterizing the course of occasions. The English East India Organization, reinforced by its monetary may and royal aspirations, tried to unite its command over the Indian subcontinent.

The last part of Tipu Ruler's life unfurled in 1798 when he wound up by and by snared in a contention with the English, known as the Fourth Old English Mysore War. The conflict ended up being a finish of long stretches of stewing strains, and it eventually prompted Tipu Ruler's downfall in 1799. His courageous endeavors to oppose frontier mastery had come at a weighty expense, and the Tiger of Mysore fell on the war zone protecting his realm.

The fall of Tipu King denoted an essential crossroads throughout the entire existence of the Indian subcontinent, implying the fading of native powers and the command of English provincial rule. The repercussions of his obstruction resonated a long ways past the boundaries of Mysore, molding the direction of India's battle for freedom in the hundreds of years that followed.

As we dive into the tradition of the Tiger of Mysore, it is fundamental to explore the subtleties of authentic translation and perceive the complex idea of Tipu King's standard. His inheritance is an embroidery woven with strings of military courage, regulatory intuition, social support, and the intricacies of exploring a time set apart by supreme desires and moving loyalties.

In the resulting sections of this investigation, we will unwind the layers of Tipu King's heritage, diving into the complexities of his tactical techniques, regulatory changes, social commitments, and the persevering through effect of his opposition against pioneer powers. The Tiger of Mysore remains as an image of resistance against mistreatment, and his inheritance keeps on enticing researchers, history specialists, and lovers the same to disentangle the rich embroidery of history that he helped shape.

Chapter 1

Rise of the Tiger

The verifiable scene of the Indian subcontinent in the eighteenth century saw the ascent of an imposing pioneer whose heritage would resound through the halls of time. Tipu Ruler, frequently alluded to as the "Tiger of Mysore," arose as a focal figure in the international chessboard of the period, his rising to control set apart by a juncture of conditions and a significant obligation to safeguarding his realm against outer powers.

Tipu King's ascent to conspicuousness unfurled against the setting of the wild political environment of the Deccan area. In 1782, following the demise of his dad, Ruler Hyder Ali, Tipu rose to the privileged position of the Realm of Mysore. The conditions of his promotion were loaded with difficulties, as the youthful ruler wound up in charge of a realm decisively situated in the midst of the contending interests of European powers.

The English East India Organization, in its quest for regional development and monetary strength, had immovably laid down a good foundation for itself as a considerable player in the Indian subcontinent. Tipu Ruler's rule harmonized with a time of uplifted strain and struggle between the Mysorean Realm and the English, making way for the wild situation that would transpire in the years to come.

The moniker "Tiger of Mysore" was not a simple sobriquet but rather an impression of Tipu King's dauntless soul and military ability. His initial a long time on the lofty position were set apart by a progression of military missions pointed toward getting the regional trustworthiness of Mysore. The Somewhat English Mysore Wars, traversing various contentions, turned into the theater where Tipu King displayed his essential brightness and unfaltering assurance to oppose outside infringements.

The First and Second Old English Mysore Wars, battled in the last option some portion of the eighteenth hundred years, established the groundwork for Tipu Ruler's standing as a considerable foe. His creative military techniques, including the utilization of rocket innovation, acquired him both reverence and dread on the front line. The conflicts with the English powers were not simply about regional questions; they epitomized a bigger battle for independence and the conservation of the social and political personality of Mysore.

As Tipu Ruler stood up to the growing reach of the English East India Organization, his administration stretched out past the war zone. He executed moderate authoritative changes pointed toward encouraging monetary turn of events and guaranteeing the government assistance of his subjects. The Tiger of Mysore was not only a tactical strategist but rather likewise a visionary ruler who perceived the significance of an efficient and effective organization in exploring the difficulties of his time.

Tipu King's standard was described by a multicultural and comprehensive methodology. Regardless of being a Muslim ruler, he showed an exceptional resilience towards strict variety, cultivating a climate where Hindus, Muslims, and Christians coincided amicably. His organization contained authorities from different strict foundations, a demonstration of his obligation to pluralism in administration.

The Deal of Mangalore in 1784 carried an impermanent break to the contention among Mysore and the English East India Organization. In any case, the uncomfortable harmony was accentuated by the fundamental pressures that stewed underneath the surface. Tipu King explored the fragile harmony between discretionary suggestions and military readiness, keenly conscious about the always present danger presented by the extending English impact.

The break demonstrated fleeting, as the international scene kept on moving, making way for the Third and Fourth Somewhat English Mysore Wars. Tipu King's obstruction against the English powers arrived at its pinnacle during the Third Somewhat English Mysore War, where he confronted the joined could of English and Maratha powers. In spite of the imposing coalition displayed against him, the Tiger of Mysore showed unrivaled mental fortitude and military astuteness.

The finish of Tipu Ruler's disobedience unfurled in 1799 during the Fourth Old English Mysore War. The English, under the order of General Sir Arthur Wellesley, blockaded the capital city of Srirangapatna. The attack ended up being an extended and burdensome issue, with Tipu King showing enduring determination despite overpowering chances. The possible fall of Srirangapatna denoted a defining moment throughout the entire existence of Mysore and the more extensive Indian subcontinent.

Tipu King's end on the war zone was not just the finish of a ruler but rather the determination of a section in the battle against pioneer control. His inheritance, complicatedly woven with strings of opposition and flexibility, turned into an image of insubordination that resounded a long ways past the boundaries of Mysore. The Tiger of Mysore's obligation to freedom and his refusal to bow before outside powers made a permanent imprint on the shared mindset of a subcontinent wrestling with the infringement of pilgrim powers.

The fall of Tipu Ruler denoted the ascendance of English predominance in the Deccan area and, likewise, the Indian subcontinent. The repercussions of his opposition reverberated through the resulting many years, affecting the direction of India's battle for autonomy in the nineteenth and twentieth hundreds of years. The Tiger of Mysore turned into an image of motivation for the people who tried to break liberated from the shackles of frontier rule and declare their right to self-assurance.

As we think about the ascent of the Tiger of Mysore, perceiving the intricacies inborn in his legacy is basic. Tipu King's standard was not without discussion, and authentic stories encompassing his rule have been dependent upon assorted translations. While he is praised as a public legend in certain quarters, others view him from the perspective of local or strict personality, featuring the nuanced idea of verifiable points of view.

The ascent of the Tiger of Mysore is a diverse story that rises above the limits of time. It incorporates military adventures, authoritative changes, social support, and the persevering through soul of opposition against magnificent powers. Tipu King's inheritance welcomes researchers, students of history, and lovers to dig into the rich embroidery of history, investigating the complexities of a time where a solitary individual, the Tiger of Mysore, remained as a defense against the tide of frontier development.

1.1 Introduction to the historical and cultural context of 18th-century Mysore.

The eighteenth 100 years in the Indian subcontinent saw a kaleidoscope of verifiable, social, and political changes, with the Realm of Mysore remaining as a lively microcosm of these changes.

Settled in the core of the Deccan district, Mysore, subject to the Wodeyar line and later King Hyder Ali and his child Tipu Ruler, arose as a point of convergence of international interest, social thriving, and obstruction against outer powers.

At the beginning of the eighteenth 100 years, the Indian subcontinent was an interwoven of different states and territories, each exploring the intricate flows of local power elements. The downfall of the Mughal Realm, when the superior power in the subcontinent, had made a power vacuum, preparing for the ascent of local powers competing for matchless quality. Mysore, arranged decisively between the Marathas in the north, the Nizam of Hyderabad toward the upper east, and the English East India Organization infringing from the south, ended up at the junction of these moving tides.

The Wodeyar line, which had managed Mysore for a really long time, confronted difficulties in keeping up with command over their domains. The eighteenth century saw inward struggle, with groups inside the regal family competing for authority. In the midst of this inward friction, the figure of King Hyder Ali arose as a powerful power, reshaping the predetermination of Mysore. His ascent denoted a takeoff from the genetic rule of the Wodeyars, introducing a period of military ability and political practicality.

Hyder Ali's rising to drive during the eighteenth century was described by a sharp comprehension of the international scene. Perceiving the infringing danger presented by the English East India Organization, he participated in a progression of military missions to protect Mysore's sway. The fights battled during his rule laid the basis for the later struggles that would characterize the tradition of his child, Tipu King.

The social milieu of eighteenth century Mysore was an embroidery woven with the strings of variety and pluralism. Mysore, similar to a large part of the Indian subcontinent, was a conjunction of different strict, phonetic, and social customs. Hinduism, Islam, and Christianity coincided agreeably, with the leaders of Mysore embracing a comprehensive way to deal with administration. The support of human expression, sciences, and strict foundations thrived, making a social renaissance that made a permanent imprint on the social texture of the realm.

Mysore's capital, Srirangapatna, turned into a focal point of social energy subject to Hyder Ali and Tipu Ruler. The illustrious court turned into a benefactor of writers, performers, and craftsmen, encouraging a climate where imagination flourished. The building scene of Srirangapatna gave testimony regarding this social flowering, with the development of royal residences, mosques, and different designs mirroring the combination of different creative practices.

As Mysore explored the difficulties presented by outside controls, the eighteenth century saw the intersection of conventional Indian military methodologies with imaginative methodologies. The utilization of rocket innovation, credited to Tipu King, became significant of Mysore's tactical ability. These progressions exhibited a sharp consciousness of the changing idea of fighting and a pledge to safeguarding the realm against the infringing powers of pioneer development.

The international chessboard of the time set up for the Somewhat English Mysore Wars, a progression of contentions that would characterize the destiny of Mysore in the late eighteenth hundred years. The English East India Organization, driven by royal aspirations and financial interests, tried to extend its impact in the Deccan locale. Mysore, under the initiative of Hyder Ali and later Tipu Ruler, arose as a considerable foe, testing the uncontrolled expansionism of the English.

The Arrangement of Mangalore in 1784, following the Second Old English Mysore War, briefly ended threats among Mysore and the English. Nonetheless, the basic strains persevered, as the two powers moved carefully and militarily in a fragile dance for strength. The international elements of the time were set apart by moving partnerships, with provincial powers recalibrating their procedures because of the developing danger scene.

The social and strict inclusivity advocated by the leaders of Mysore was not without its intricacies. While the realm flourished as a mixture of different customs, the mind boggling interchange of strict and political elements added layers of subtlety to the verifiable story. Tipu King's standard, specifically, has been the subject of assorted translations, with discusses fixating on the idea of his strict strategies and their effect on the social texture of Mysore.

The downfall of the Wodeyar line and the ensuing ascent of Hyder Ali and Tipu King denoted an extraordinary period throughout the entire existence of Mysore. The realm, once bound to local elements, turned into a player in the more extensive international venue of the Indian subcontinent. The tradition of Tipu King, the Tiger of Mysore, typifies the soul of obstruction against frontier powers and stays an image of boldness that rises above local and social limits.

In the following investigation of eighteenth century Mysore, we will dive further into the tactical procedures, regulatory changes, social commitments, and the persevering through effect of the Somewhat English Mysore Wars. The many-sided embroidery of this verifiable and social setting welcomes us to disentangle the intricacies of a former time, where the Realm of Mysore remained at the intersection of custom and change, exploring the flows of progress with versatility and backbone.

1.2 Early life and upbringing of Tipu Sultan.

The early existence of Tipu King, the famous Tiger of Mysore, unfurls against the setting of the eighteenth century Deccan locale, a period set apart by political complexities and moving partnerships. Brought into the world in 1751 in Devanahalli, a town close to introduce day Bangalore, Tipu Ruler, initially named King Fateh Ali Sahab Tipu, was the oldest child of Ruler Hyder Ali and Fatima Fakhr-un-Nisa.

All along, Tipu Ruler's life was saturated with the milieu of political aspiration and military methodology. His dad, Hyder Ali, a tactical leader in the multitude of the Wodeyar tradition in Mysore, rose to unmistakable quality through a blend of military expertise and political sharpness. Hyder Ali's climb to drive denoted a takeoff from the conventional rule of the Wodeyars, and his endeavors to unite command over Mysore laid the basis for the heritage acquired by Tipu King.

Tipu Ruler's childhood was affected by the tactical ethos of his dad's profession. Since early on, he was presented to the afflictions of military preparation and vital reasoning. The turbulent political environment of the Deccan, with outer dangers from the English East India Organization and provincial opponents, required a powerful protection device. Accordingly, Tipu King's early stages were molded by the basic of planning for the difficulties that lay ahead.

Hyder Ali's tactical missions against the Marathas, the Nizam of Hyderabad, and the English East India Organization gave Tipu King important experiences into the elements of provincial power legislative issues. These missions not just presented him to the craft of fighting yet in addition saturated him with a profound feeling of obligation toward the safeguard of Mysore. The youthful ruler's schooling was not restricted to ordinary subjects; it enveloped an exhaustive comprehension of military technique, administration, and the international complexities of the time.

Tipu Ruler's relationship with his dad, Hyder Ali, was urgent in molding his perspective and way to deal with authority. Hyder Ali's tactical triumphs and discretionary moving turned into a wellspring of motivation for the youthful ruler. The familial connection among father and child was invigorated by a common vision of shielding Mysore against outer dangers. Tipu King, in numerous ways, was the main beneficiary of the political tradition of his dad as well as the overseer of a strong soul of obstruction against royal powers.

The demise of Hyder Ali in 1782 denoted a critical crossroads in Tipu Ruler's life. At 31 years old, he climbed to the privileged position of Mysore, acquiring a realm entangled in the complex international battles of the time. The progress from sovereign to ruler requested military keenness as well as a nuanced comprehension of administration and strategy.

Tipu Ruler's initial a very long time on the lofty position were portrayed by a quick and confident combination of force as he tried to explore the unpredictable trap of partnerships and contentions that characterized the Deccan district.

The multi-layered nature of Tipu Ruler's initial life reached out past the domain of governmental issues and military undertakings. His strict character, as a Muslim ruler in an overwhelmingly Hindu realm, added layers of intricacy to his standard. Tipu Ruler, nonetheless, embraced a comprehensive way to deal with administration, displaying a regard for strict variety. He selected authorities from different strict foundations to enter positions in his organization, encouraging a climate of pluralism inside the realm.

The managerial changes started by Tipu King mirrored a visionary way to deal with administration. He tried to modernize the regulatory hardware, acquainting measures with smooth out tax assessment, further develop foundation, and improve the productivity of the state contraption. His obligation to monetary turn of events and mechanical development reflected the changing elements of the eighteenth 100 years, where conventional designs were giving way to additional moderate and concentrated frameworks.

Tipu Ruler's support of artistic expression and sciences further highlighted his obligation to social thriving. Srirangapatna, the capital of Mysore, turned into an energetic focal point of scholarly and creative movement during his standard. Writers, performers, and researchers tracked down support in his court, adding to a social renaissance that rose above strict and etymological limits. The engineering scene of Srirangapatna mirrored this social liveliness, with the development of castles and designs that mixed different creative practices.

While Tipu Ruler's initial a very long time on the privileged position were set apart by strategic suggestions and endeavors to explore the mind boggling embroidery of provincial governmental issues, the phantom of contention with the English East India Organization posed a potential threat. The Deal of Mangalore in 1784, which briefly ended threats, gave a concise break, however the hidden strains endured. The ensuing years saw Tipu King participated in a sensitive difficult exercise, looking to protect Mysore's sway while haggling with outside powers.

The Tiger of Mysore's initial life and childhood, established in the cauldron of military preparation and political interest, established the groundwork for an initiative style described by strength, development, and an undaunted obligation to protecting his realm. The examples gained from his dad's missions, the perplexing exchange of strict and social elements, and the basic of administration in an impacting world all met to shape the direction of Tipu King's standard.

As we dive further into the existence of Tipu King, we will unwind the layers of his tactical techniques, political undertakings, social commitments, and the getting through tradition of opposition against frontier powers. The Tiger of Mysore, rising up out of the pot of his initial years, remains as an image of insubordination against mistreatment and a pioneer whose effect rises above the bounds of his time.

1.3 The political landscape and the ascension to the throne.

The eighteenth century political scene of the Indian subcontinent was portrayed by a complicated transaction of local powers, moving coalitions, and the infringement of European royal powers. Against this background, the Realm of Mysore arose as a huge player in the Deccan locale, and the rising of Tipu Ruler to the lofty position denoted a urgent second in the political elements of the time.

The Wodeyar line had customarily managed over Mysore, yet by the mid-eighteenth hundred years, the district confronted inside conflict and outer dangers that would reshape its fate. In this specific circumstance, Ruler Hyder Ali, a tactical leader in the help of the Wodeyars, jumping all over the chance to rise to control. His tactical ability and political discernment moved him to a position where he turned into the true leader of Mysore, making way for the ascent of Tipu King.

Ruler Hyder Ali's climb to control was not without its difficulties. The political scene of the Deccan was set apart by the desires of provincial powers like the Marathas and the Nizam of Hyderabad, as well as the developing impact of the English East India Organization. Hyder Ali's initial missions were coordinated towards getting Mysore against outside dangers and solidifying his command over the realm.

The changing elements of force in the district prompted a takeoff from the genetic rule of the Wodeyars. King Hyder Ali's ascent addressed a shift towards a more even minded and strategic way to deal with administration. His prosperity on the combat zone and his capacity to explore the intricacies of territorial legislative issues situated him as a focal figure in the unfurling show of eighteenth century Deccan legislative issues.

The international scene of the time set up for Hyder Ali's commitment with the English East India Organization. The organization, driven by supreme desires and monetary interests, tried to extend its impact in the Indian subcontinent. The conflict of interests among Mysore and the English brought about a progression of struggles known as the Old English Mysore Battles, with Hyder Ali at the very front of the opposition against provincial infringement.

Hyder Ali's tactical missions against the English were portrayed by essential brightness and creative strategies. His initial achievements in fights, for example, the Clash of Pollilur in 1780 displayed his capacity to challenge the regular military procedures utilized by the English. The contention with the English East India Organization turned into a characterizing element of Hyder Ali's standard and made way for his child Tipu Ruler to acquire a realm dug in the battle against pioneer powers.

The demise of Ruler Hyder Ali in 1782 denoted a basic point in the political direction of Mysore. With Hyder Ali's passing, Tipu King, his oldest child, rose to the privileged position. The conditions encompassing Tipu King's climb were full of difficulties, both inward and outer. The youthful ruler ended up in charge of a realm entrapped in the intricacies of provincial power elements and the determined expansionism of the English.

Tipu Ruler's initial a long time on the high position were set apart by a quick and self-assured union of force. The ghost of contention with the English posed a potential threat, and Tipu King, acquiring his dad's obligation to opposing provincial powers, confronted the considerable undertaking of protecting Mysore's sway. The realm, currently entangled in the Somewhat English Mysore Wars, remained as a defense against the unrestrained extension of the English East India Organization.

The political scene that Tipu King explored was formed by the international competitions of the time. The Marathas, the Nizam of Hyderabad, and the English East India Organization competed for strength, each looking to attest its impact over the Deccan locale. Tipu Ruler, with a sharp consciousness of the moving tides of force, participated in strategic suggestions and military readiness to protect Mysore's independence.

The Settlement of Mangalore in 1784, following the Second Old English Mysore War, carried an impermanent suspension to threats among Mysore and the English. Be that as it may, the fundamental strains endured, and the resulting years saw Tipu King's sensitive dance among strategy and military moving. The international elements were liquid, with unions moving and outside pressures escalating.

Tipu King's rising to the high position not just denoted a continuation of the obstruction against frontier powers yet additionally addressed a progress in the style of administration. His initial years saw a promise to regulatory changes pointed toward cultivating monetary turn of events and mechanical development inside the realm. Tipu King, similar as his dad, perceived the significance of a vigorous safeguard device and an efficient organization in exploring the difficulties of the time.

The Tiger of Mysore's political insight was not bound to the combat zone; it stretched out to the domain of tact. Tipu Ruler participated in dealings with different provincial powers, endeavoring to explore the complicated snare of collusions and competitions. His endeavors to manufacture conciliatory ties were grounded in a practical comprehension of the requirement for key unions to offset the staggering could of the English.

The complex political scene of eighteenth century Mysore, set apart by the conflict of territorial powers and the infringement of magnificent powers, set up for Tipu King's standard. His rising to the high position addressed a continuation of the obstruction against outer control and a pledge to protecting the independence of Mysore. The Tiger of Mysore's initial a very long time in power were a demonstration of his capacity to explore the intricacies of international relations, military methodology, and administration, laying the foundation for the turbulent occasions that would characterize his heritage.

Chapter 2

The Sword of Islam

The designation "The Sword of Islam" exemplifies the tradition of Tipu Ruler, the Tiger of Mysore, and his immovable obligation to protecting his realm against outside powers during the late eighteenth hundred years. This title reflects Tipu Ruler's tactical ability as well as highlights the crossing point of his Islamic personality with the political and social scene of the time.

Tipu King's relationship with Islam was a focal part of his character, impacting his own convictions as well as forming the strategies of his standard. Naturally introduced to a Muslim family, Tipu Ruler acquired a realm settled in the different strict and social texture of the Indian subcontinent. His initial years were saturated with the practices of Islam, and as he rose to the privileged position, this strict personality became entwined with the difficulties and amazing open doors that characterized his rule.

The Blade of Islam's tactical missions against the English East India Organization and other provincial powers were not simply essential moves; they were instilled with a feeling of strict obligation. Tipu King considered himself to be a protector of Islam even with apparent dangers from frontier controls and tried to oppose what he saw as an infringement on the power of Muslim-controlled domains.

The international scene of eighteenth century India was set apart by the desires of European pioneer powers, and the English East India Organization, specifically, represented an impressive test to native rulers. Tipu King's obligation to Islam showed in his obstruction against provincial powers as well as in his collaborations with other local powers, where strict contemplations frequently assumed a part in forming coalitions and hatreds.

The utilization of the title "The Blade of Islam" implies Tipu Ruler's arrangement with a more extensive Islamic character that rose above the lines of his realm. His standard harmonized with a period when different Islamic states and realms had declined, leaving a void that pioneer powers looked to fill. Tipu King's endeavors to oppose this tide were, in his view, a sign of his obligation as a Muslim ruler to safeguard the interests of the ummah (the worldwide Muslim people group).

Tipu King's tactical missions against the English East India Organization, frequently alluded to as the Somewhat English Mysore Wars, were educated by a profound sense regarding strict obligation. The Skirmish of Pollilur in 1780, where Hyder Ali and Tipu King scored an unequivocal triumph against the English, turned into a vital second that built up the possibility of a noble battle against pioneer powers. The utilization of cutting edge military innovations, including the renowned Mysorean rockets, displayed a mix of military development and strict enthusiasm.

As "The Blade of Islam," Tipu King looked for partnerships with other Muslim rulers, perceiving the potential strength that a unified front could bring against the normal foe. His conciliatory suggestions to the Ottoman Realm, the leaders of Afghanistan, and, surprisingly, the French, were grounded in a common Islamic personality that rose above provincial and social contrasts. Tipu King imagined a container Islamic union that could by and large oppose the infringements of pioneer powers in the Indian subcontinent.

The Tiger of Mysore's commitment with other Islamic powers was not without its difficulties. The international real factors of the time implied that unions were in many cases sober minded, and the moving sands of force constrained rulers to reevaluate their affiliations. Tipu Ruler's suggestions to the Ottoman Realm, for example, didn't bring about the ideal military help, featuring the complicated idea of strategic relations in the eighteenth 100 years.

Past the war zone, Tipu King's standard was set apart by a joining of Islamic standards into the organization of Mysore. His obligation to equity, decency, and the government assistance of his subjects repeated Islamic standards of administration. Tipu Ruler's organization included authorities from different strict foundations, mirroring a comprehensive methodology that tried to blend assorted networks inside the realm.

Tipu King's money, engraved with Islamic expressions and images, further exemplified the joining of his strict character into the texture of his standard. The utilization of Islamic calligraphy and themes on coins was not just an emblematic signal; it was an intentional articulation of Tipu King's obligation to his confidence and an impression of the Islamic social milieu that formed his perspective.

The Sword of Islam's standard was not without its discussions in regards to his treatment of non-Muslim subjects. A few verifiable records propose that Tipu Ruler's strategies toward Hindus were described by compulsion and constrained changes. Notwithstanding, the nuanced the truth is dependent upon verifiable translation, with discusses encompassing the degree of strict resistance and inclusivity during his rule.

Tipu King's associations with non-Muslim people group were complicated and changed. While occasions of strict mistreatment have been refered to, there were likewise examples of strict pluralism inside his organization. The sanctuary at Srirangapatna, which Tipu King is accepted to have belittled, remains as a demonstration of the concurrence of various strict networks during his standard.

The moniker "The Blade of Islam" welcomes examination and investigation of Tipu King's inheritance according to various viewpoints. As far as some might be concerned, he stays a bold safeguard of Islam who opposed pioneer powers and looked to join Muslim powers against a shared adversary. For other people, particularly taking into account the intricacies of his standard, his inheritance is more nuanced, including a blend of military courage, regulatory developments, and strict strategies that have been dependent upon verifiable discussion.

The downfall of Mysore under Tipu King's standard arrived at a basic crossroads with the Fourth Somewhat English Mysore War. Not entirely set in stone to quell the Tiger of Mysore, blockaded Srirangapatna in 1799. The fall of the capital denoted the finish of Tipu Ruler's obstruction and his possible demise on the war zone.

The Blade of Islam's inheritance stays a subject of interest and contention. His obligation to Islam, as reflected in his tactical missions, strategic undertakings, and regulatory arrangements, highlights the intricacy of his standard. Tipu King's endeavors to manufacture a container Islamic partnership against provincial powers, while confronting the difficulties of commonsense international relations, represent the diverse idea of his commitment with his strict personality.

In the more extensive setting of Indian history, Tipu King's opposition against frontier powers addresses a huge section in the battle against unfamiliar control. His heritage, as "The Blade of Islam," rises above territorial and strict limits, igniting conversations about the crossing points of confidence, administration, and military obstruction in the perplexing scene of eighteenth century India. The Tiger of Mysore, with his sword brought up with regards to his realm and confidence, stays a persevering through figure whose effect resonates through the records of history.

2.1 Exploration of Tipu Sultan's religious beliefs and policies.

Investigating the strict convictions and strategies of Tipu King, the Tiger of Mysore, gives a nuanced comprehension of a ruler whose character was unpredictably woven with his obligation to Islam. Naturally introduced to a Muslim family in the eighteenth hundred years, Tipu Ruler's reign unfurled in a time of critical political, social, and strict changes in the Indian subcontinent.

Tipu Ruler's strict convictions were well established in the precepts of Islam. His childhood in a Muslim family and the tactical ethos that formed his initial years imparted in him a solid feeling of Islamic character. As he climbed to the lofty position of Mysore in 1782, his strict convictions became laced with the difficulties of overseeing a realm confronting outside dangers from pioneer powers and provincial opponents.

The Tiger of Mysore's strict convictions appeared in different parts of his standard, including his tactical missions, authoritative approaches, and cooperations with various strict networks. His title, "King," meant the two his political power and his situation as a Muslim ruler, repeating the tradition of Islamic administration in the Indian subcontinent.

Tipu Ruler's tactical missions against the English East India Organization, frequently alluded to as the Somewhat English Mysore Wars, were not exclusively international moves but rather were pervaded with a feeling of strict obligation. The Clash of Pollilur in 1780, where Tipu Ruler and his dad King Hyder Ali got a definitive triumph against the English, was viewed as a justification of their obligation to Islam despite saw dangers from pilgrim powers.

The utilization of cutting edge military advances, for example, the prestigious Mysorean rockets, exhibited Tipu Ruler's tactical development as well as his assurance to protect his realm with the apparatuses accessible to him. These tactical progressions were not separated from his strict personality; they addressed a combination of key need and a confidence in the honorableness of the reason.

Tipu Ruler's commitment with other Muslim powers mirrored his craving to manufacture a unified front against the infringements of pioneer powers. His political suggestions to the Ottoman Domain, the leaders of Afghanistan, and, surprisingly, the French were grounded in a common Islamic personality that rose above local and social contrasts. Tipu King imagined a container Islamic partnership that could by and large oppose the magnificent plans of European powers in the Indian subcontinent.

The coordination of Islamic standards into the organization of Mysore was an outstanding part of Tipu King's standard. His obligation to equity, decency, and the government assistance of his subjects repeated Islamic standards of administration. While his strategies have been dependent upon authentic discussions and understandings, Tipu Ruler's organization included authorities from different strict foundations, mirroring a comprehensive methodology that looked to fit assorted networks inside the realm.

Tipu Ruler's money is in many cases refered to as an outflow of his strict character. The engravings on his begets included Islamic sayings and images, exhibiting an intentional coordination of his confidence into the monetary and representative parts of his standard. The utilization of Islamic calligraphy and themes on coins was not just an emblematic motion; it was an unmistakable portrayal of Tipu Ruler's obligation to his confidence and a statement of the Islamic social milieu that formed his perspective.

In any case, Tipu Ruler's strict strategies and their effect on non-Muslim people group have been a subject of verifiable discussion. A few verifiable records propose that his strategies toward Hindus were portrayed by intimidation and constrained transformations. While occasions of strict oppression have been refered to, the nuanced the truth is dependent upon authentic understanding, and discussions encompassing the degree of strict resistance and inclusivity during his rule persevere.

Tipu Ruler's connections with non-Muslim people group were complicated and fluctuated. The sanctuary at Srirangapatna, accepted to have been disparaged by Tipu King, remains as a demonstration of the conjunction of various strict networks during his standard. Be that as it may, verifiable records likewise demonstrate examples of strictly roused activities, prompting banters about the harmony between strict inclusivity and the attestation of Islamic personality.

The moniker "The Sword of Islam" embodies Tipu King's job as a safeguard of his confidence even with apparent dangers from pilgrim powers. In any case, the title likewise welcomes examination of the intricacies inborn in his strict approaches and the exchange between administration, military methodology, and confidence. Tipu King's obligation to Islam was a main thrust in his opposition against outside mastery, forming the direction of his standard and making a permanent imprint on the verifiable story.

The downfall of Mysore under Tipu King's standard arrived at a basic crossroads with the Fourth Old English Mysore War. Still up in the air to curb the Tiger of Mysore, assaulted Srirangapatna in 1799. The fall of the capital denoted the finish of Tipu Ruler's opposition and his possible passing on the war zone. The finishing up part of his life further filled banters about the idea of his strict convictions and the effect of his approaches on the assorted strict networks inside his realm.

In the more extensive setting of Indian history, Tipu King's heritage stays a subject of interest and discussion. His obligation to Islam, as reflected in his tactical missions, discretionary undertakings, and regulatory approaches, highlights the intricacy of his standard. Tipu King's endeavors to produce a dish Islamic coalition against provincial powers, while confronting the difficulties of realistic international relations, represent the complex idea of his commitment with his strict personality.

As we investigate Tipu Ruler's strict convictions and arrangements, it becomes obvious that his heritage is both rich and challenged. The Sword of Islam's standard addresses a critical section in the battle against unfamiliar mastery, and his effect resounds through the chronicles of history. Tipu Ruler's obligation to Islam, his tactical fearlessness, and the intricacies of his administration welcome researchers, history specialists, and fans to dive further into the complex embroidery of a period where confidence, governmental issues, and personality merged in the cauldron of eighteenth century India.

2.2 Military strategies and innovations during Tipu's reign.

Tipu Ruler, the Tiger of Mysore, is praised not just for his relentless opposition against pilgrim controls yet additionally for his tactical intuition and creative systems. His rule during the late eighteenth century was set apart by a progression of contentions with the English East India Organization, known as the Somewhat English Mysore Wars. Analyzing Tipu King's tactical techniques and developments gives knowledge into the dynamic and versatile nature of his way to deal with shielding Mysore.

Key to Tipu Ruler's tactical system was his capacity to coordinate customary

Indian fighting strategies with imaginative and present day techniques. Naturally introduced to a family with a tactical foundation, he acquired an inheritance formed by the essential bits of knowledge of his dad, Ruler Hyder Ali. The tactical ethos that pervaded his childhood impacted the direction of his standard, and Tipu Ruler's methodologies bore the engraving of a commandant knowledgeable in the intricacies of eighteenth century fighting.

One of the most remarkable elements of Tipu King's tactical advancement was the utilization of rocket innovation. The Mysorean rockets, frequently alluded to as "Tipu's Rockets," became significant of his tactical ability. These rockets were mechanically best in class for their experience as well as represented a takeoff from ordinary strategies for fighting. Tipu King perceived the competitive edge of rocketry, utilizing it in fights against the English and other territorial powers.

The rockets used by Tipu Ruler were intended for both hostile and guarded purposes. They went from more modest, portable rockets utilized on the front line to bigger, all the more impressive rockets with expanded ranges. The rockets were compelling against both infantry and mounted force, exhibiting the flexibility of this creative military innovation. The utilization of rockets during the Skirmish of Pollilur in 1780, where the Mysoreans scored a huge triumph against the English, featured the effect of this flighty weaponry.

Past rocketry, Tipu King's tactical developments stretched out to the association and preparing of his military. He modernized the tactical framework of Mysore, presenting restrained preparing techniques and normalized hardware. The utilization of guns, gunnery, and infantry in facilitated moves mirrored an essential familiarity with the changing elements of fighting in the eighteenth hundred years.

Tipu Ruler's military, known as the Fauj-I-Khas, was a considerable power on the combat zone as well as an image of his obligation to military greatness. The troopers of the Fauj-I-Khas went through thorough preparation, and their faithfulness to Tipu Ruler was built up through a feeling of common perspective and character. This professionalization of the military, combined with creative advancements, improved the adequacy of Mysore's protection against outside dangers.

Decisively, Tipu Ruler embraced a proactive way to deal with shielding Mysore's power. Perceiving the expansionist desires of the English East India Organization, he participated in a progression of military missions to counter their infringement. The fights battled during his rule, including the four Old English Mysore Wars, were described by a mix of regular and capricious strategies.

The Skirmish of Pollilur in 1780 stands apart as a urgent second in Tipu King's tactical missions. The successful utilization of rockets, alongside essential situating and facilitated troop developments, brought about a reverberating triumph for the Mysoreans. This fight not just displayed the tactical developments of Tipu King yet additionally showed his capacity to adjust and counter the ordinary techniques utilized by the English.

Be that as it may, military achievement was not generally steady for Tipu Ruler.

The fluctuating fortunes of war, moving collusions, and the imposing could of the English East India Organization made a difficult and dynamic combat zone. The Deal of Mangalore in 1784, following the Second Somewhat English Mysore War, gave a brief relief, however hidden pressures continued, prompting resulting clashes.

Tipu Ruler's tactical systems were not restricted to cautious activities; he likewise sought after conciliatory drives to produce collusions against pilgrim powers. His effort to other provincial powers and endeavors to make a container Islamic collusion were key moves to offset the staggering could of the English. While these conciliatory undertakings were not generally effective, they reflected Tipu Ruler's familiarity with the international complexities of the time.

The fall of Srirangapatna in 1799 denoted the zenith of Tipu King's tactical opposition against the English. The Fourth Somewhat English Mysore War, filled by an intersection of international variables, saw the blockading of his capital and Tipu Ruler's passing on the war zone. The finish of his rule highlighted the difficulties of supporting military advancements and methodologies against the constant expansionism of pioneer powers.

The tradition of Tipu King's tactical procedures reaches out past the authentic account of his time. The creative utilization of rocket innovation, the professionalization of the military, and the essential prescience in expecting and countering pilgrim dangers add to his standing as a tactical visionary. The Tiger of Mysore's way to deal with fighting exhibited a mix of custom and development, mirroring a comprehension of the developing idea of contention in the eighteenth 100 years.

The effect of Tipu Ruler's tactical techniques resonates through the chronicles of history, affecting resulting ages of military masterminds and tacticians. The joining of rocketry, restrained preparing, and a versatile way to deal with fighting made a permanent imprint on the more extensive direction of military history in the Indian subcontinent.

As we dig into the investigation of Tipu Ruler's tactical procedures and developments, it becomes clear that his heritage stretches out past the combat zone. The Tiger of Mysore, through his visionary way to deal with military issues, left a getting through engrave on the craft of battle in the Indian subcontinent, moving ages to come. The unique combination of custom and development in his tactical missions mirrors a pioneer who, despite considerable difficulties, tried to protect his realm with vital brightness and resolute assurance.

2.3 Relations with neighboring states and the British East India Company.

Tipu Ruler's rule during the late eighteenth century unfurled against a complex international background, portrayed by moving collusions, territorial contentions, and the infringement of European frontier powers. His relations with adjoining states and, all the more noticeably, the English East India Organization, assumed a significant part in forming the direction of Mysore's fate. Analyzing these strategic elements gives knowledge into the difficulties and amazing open doors that characterized Tipu Ruler's standard.

Mysore's closeness to strong neighbors, like the Marathas and the Nizam of Hyderabad, set up for unpredictable strategic moves. The Marathas, with their extensive regional desires, looked to declare predominance over the Deccan district. The Nizam of Hyderabad, then again, was a central member with vital interests adjusting or clashing with those of Mysore at different places.

Tipu King, conscious of the local power elements, participated in strategic suggestions to explore the multifaceted snare of unions and competitions. His way to deal with adjoining states mirrored a mix of practicality and vital prescience. The moving sands of collusions implied that Tipu Ruler needed to recalibrate his political systems in view of the advancing international scene.

One of the eminent examples of Tipu King's discretionary moving was his commitment with the Marathas. The Maratha-Mysore relations wavered among participation and struggle. Tipu King, perceiving the shared advantage of a stable Deccan, looked for coalitions with the Marathas against normal enemies, including the English East India Organization. Notwithstanding, the liquid idea of collusions in the eighteenth century implied that these organizations were many times transient, with interests separating and joining in view of the international setting.

The Nizam of Hyderabad, one more critical player in the Deccan, presented the two open doors and difficulties for Tipu King. The Nizam's arrangement with Mysore could give an impressive front against outer dangers, especially from the English. Alternately, the Nizam's advantages some of the time clashed with those of Mysore, prompting times of stressed relations and, surprisingly, military showdowns.

The Second Old English Mysore War (1780-1784) brought the elements of local unions into more keen concentration. Tipu Ruler, confronting the expansionist plans of the English East India Organization, looked to produce collusions with the Marathas and the Nizam against the shared adversary. The Settlement of Gajendragad in 1787 formalized the partnership between Mysore, the Marathas, and the Nizam, flagging an uncommon snapshot of provincial solidarity against pilgrim powers.

Be that as it may, the life span of these unions was restricted, and the moving loyalties among the territorial powers kept on influencing Tipu Ruler's strategic math. The Deal of Gajendragad was trailed by times of relative strength and reestablished threats, mirroring the liquid idea of coalitions in eighteenth century India.

Tipu Ruler's commitment with the English East India Organization, be that as it may, was a characterizing part of his unfamiliar relations. The Old English Mysore Wars, traversing a very long while, denoted the extreme battle among Mysore and the extending pioneer power. The English, driven by financial interests and royal desires, looked to state command over the Indian subcontinent, and Mysore, under Tipu Ruler, arose as an impressive deterrent to their arrangements.

The Primary Old English Mysore War (1767-1769) set up for the extended clash among Mysore and the English East India Organization. The underlying threats were established in regional debates and clashing interests. Tipu King's dad, Ruler Hyder Ali, started military missions against the English, establishing the groundwork for Tipu Ruler's later showdowns.

The Settlement of Madras in 1769 closed the Principal Somewhat English Mysore War, however it didn't determine the hidden strains. The international scene stayed full of rivalry, and Tipu Ruler, after rising to the privileged position, confronted the considerable test of guarding Mysore against the constant expansionism of the English.

The Second Somewhat English Mysore War (1780-1784) saw Tipu Ruler's aggressive endeavors to manufacture a unified front against the English. The coalitions with the Marathas and the Nizam, as epitomized in the Deal of Gajendragad, tried to make a local offset to pioneer powers. The contention, set apart by the Skirmish of Pollilur and different commitment, displayed Tipu King's tactical discernment in any case finished with the Arrangement of Mangalore in 1784.

The impermanent end of threats gave a short reprieve, yet the fundamental pressures continued. The resulting years saw Tipu Ruler taking part in a fragile difficult exercise, exploring the intricacies of provincial legislative issues and outer dangers. The Deal of Mangalore, while offering a time of relative security, didn't stamp the finish of threats, as the English East India Organization kept on holding onto desires of enslaving Mysore.

The Third Somewhat English Mysore War (1790-1792) unfurled against the scenery of recharged threats among Mysore and the English. Tipu King's endeavors to oppose provincial powers were met with a considerable English reaction. The Arrangement of Seringapatam in 1792, which finished up the conflict, forced huge regional and monetary concessions on Mysore. The deficiency of domain, including significant strongholds and key locales, denoted a mishap for Tipu Ruler.

The Fourth Old English Mysore War (1798-1799) ended up being the finish of the contention among Mysore and the English East India Organization. The international real factors, combined with Tipu Ruler's obstruction against frontier powers, prompted the attack of Srirangapatna in 1799. The fall of the capital denoted the finish of Tipu King's standard and his passing on the war zone.

Tipu Ruler's strategic undertakings were not exclusively restricted to military collusions and clashes. His effort reached out to other Muslim powers, mirroring a more extensive vision of dish Islamic fortitude. His correspondence with the Ottoman Domain, endeavors to lay out attaches with the leaders of Afghanistan, and discretionary suggestions to the French were grounded in a common Islamic character that rose above local limits.

Notwithstanding, these political drives confronted difficulties, and the international real factors of the time frequently muddled Tipu Ruler's endeavors to fashion a strong skillet Islamic front. The Ottoman Domain, while communicating fortitude, didn't offer the tactical help that Tipu Ruler looked for. The moving partnerships and clashing interests among Muslim powers reflected the intricacies of political relations in the eighteenth hundred years.

Tipu Ruler's relations with adjoining states and the English East India Organization uncover the mind boggling woven artwork of eighteenth century Indian international affairs. The political scene, set apart by liquid partnerships, provincial competitions, and the infringement of European powers, requested a nuanced and versatile methodology. Tipu King, as a ruler keenly conscious about these intricacies, explored the difficulties with a mix of sober mindedness, key prescience, and a guarantee to safeguarding Mysore's power.

The Tiger of Mysore's strategic inheritance stays a subject of verifiable examination and understanding. His endeavors to fashion unions against provincial powers, draw in with adjoining states, and venture a skillet Islamic vision epitomize the multi-layered nature of his unfamiliar relations. The Old English Mysore Battles, specifically, stand as a demonstration of the persevering battle between a territorial power and the extending could of the English East India Organization, with Tipu King arising as a focal figure in this verifiable show.

As we investigate Tipu King's conciliatory commitment, it becomes apparent that his inheritance stretches out past military obstruction. The Tiger of Mysore, in exploring the mind boggling flows of provincial legislative issues, made a permanent imprint on the verifiable story of eighteenth century India. His communications with adjoining states and the English East India Organization mirror a pioneer who, notwithstanding considerable difficulties, looked to guard his realm through a mix of military procedure, collusions, and strategic insight.

Chapter 3

Mysorean Wars

The Mysorean Wars, traversing a period from the late eighteenth 100 years to the mid nineteenth 100 years, were a progression of contentions that unfurled in the Indian subcontinent, principally including the Realm of Mysore and the English East India Organization. These conflicts, otherwise called the Somewhat English Mysore Wars, denoted a basic part in the international scene of the time, with Tipu Ruler, the Tiger of Mysore, arising as a focal figure in the opposition against pioneer powers. The perplexing embroidery of the Mysorean Wars uncovers the conflict of provincial powers, moving coalitions, and the determined expansionism of the English in the Indian subcontinent.

The underlying foundations of the Mysorean Wars can be followed back to the changing elements of eighteenth century India. The downfall of the Mughal Domain made a power vacuum, prompting the rise of provincial powers competing for predominance. Mysore, under the initiative of Ruler Hyder Ali, arose as a huge player in the Deccan locale. Hyder Ali's tactical ability and political keenness impelled him to a position where he turned into the true leader of Mysore, making way for the contentions that would follow.

The Primary Old English Mysore War (1767-1769) denoted the underlying showdown among Mysore and the English East India Organization. The contention was established in regional debates and clashing monetary interests. Ruler Hyder Ali, perceiving the danger presented by the growing English impact, started military missions against the English. The conflict finished up with the Deal of Madras in 1769, yet the basic pressures stayed unsettled, laying the basis for resulting threats.

The Second Somewhat English Mysore War (1780-1784) was a crucial second in the Mysorean Wars and unfurled against the setting of moving coalitions and international intricacies. Tipu Ruler, following his dad Hyder Ali's demise in 1782, rose to the lofty position of Mysore and confronted the considerable test of protecting the realm against the English. The contention saw Tipu King's endeavors to manufacture collusions with provincial powers, including the Marathas and the Nizam of Hyderabad, against the normal foe.

The Skirmish of Pollilur in 1780, an unequivocal commitment during the Second Somewhat English Mysore War, exhibited Tipu Ruler's tactical brightness and the powerful utilization of Mysorean rockets. The Mysoreans scored a huge triumph against the English, underlining the creative military techniques utilized by Tipu King. In spite of the strategic victories, the conflict closed with the Settlement of Mangalore in 1784, giving a transitory suspension of threats.

The break between the Second and Third Old English Mysore Wars was set apart by conciliatory moving, moving unions, and the intricacies of provincial legislative issues. Tipu King, perceiving the requirement for a unified front against the English, looked for partnerships with the Marathas and the Nizam. Nonetheless, the liquid idea of collusions in eighteenth century India implied that these associations were many times fleeting, with interests separating and combining in light of the international setting.

The Third Somewhat English Mysore War (1790-1792) saw reestablished threats among Mysore and the English East India Organization. Tipu King, confronting an imposing English reaction, attempted to keep up with the collusions with the Marathas and the Nizam. The contention brought about the Settlement of Seringapatam in 1792, forcing huge regional and monetary concessions on Mysore. The deficiency of key locales denoted a difficulty for Tipu Ruler and set up for the last a conflict in the Mysorean Wars.

The Fourth Somewhat English Mysore War (1798-1799) unfurled against the background of elevated pressures and Tipu Ruler's proceeded with obstruction against pilgrim powers. The international real factors, combined with the English East India Organization's assurance to stifle the Tiger of Mysore, prompted the attack of Srirangapatna in 1799. The fall of the capital denoted the finish of Tipu King's standard and his passing on the front line.

The Mysorean Wars were portrayed by an intersection of military techniques, political suggestions, and the conflict of local powers. Tipu King's job as a tactical leader, representative, and legislator became integral to the story of these contentions. His obligation to shielding Mysore's power against outside dangers and his imaginative military systems left a getting through influence on the verifiable account of eighteenth century India.

The imaginative military strategies utilized by Tipu Ruler during the Mysorean Wars, especially the utilization of rocket innovation, displayed a mix of custom and development. The Mysorean rockets, frequently alluded to as "Tipu's Rockets," became meaningful of his tactical ability. These rockets were mechanically exceptional for their experience as well as represented a takeoff from regular techniques for fighting. The Skirmish of Pollilur in 1780, where the Mysoreans scored a critical triumph against the English, featured the effect of this flighty weaponry.

The conciliatory component of the Mysorean Wars added one more layer of intricacy to the struggles. Tipu King's commitment with adjoining states, like the Marathas and the Nizam, mirrored the multifaceted trap of partnerships and contentions in eighteenth century India. The Deal of Gajendragad in 1787, formalizing a partnership against the English, exemplified Tipu King's endeavors to make a unified front even with outer dangers. In any case, the life span of these unions was restricted, and the liquid idea of territorial governmental issues implied that interests could wander, prompting moving loyalties.

Tipu Ruler's relations with the English East India Organization, particularly during the Second and Third Old English Mysore Wars, characterized the course of the contentions. The English, driven by royal desires and financial interests, tried to extend their impact in the Indian subcontinent. Tipu King's opposition against pilgrim powers exhibited his assurance to protect Mysore's independence. The Settlement of Mangalore in 1784 and the Arrangement of Seringapatam in 1792 gave impermanent breaks however didn't determine the fundamental strains.

The Fourth Old English Mysore War, finishing in the attack of Srirangapatna, denoted the finish of Tipu King's standard and the proper addition of Mysore by the English East India Organization. The international scene of the Indian subcontinent went through a huge change, with the pilgrim power uniting its impact over immense regions.

The tradition of the Mysorean Wars reaches out past the verifiable story of the struggles. Tipu Ruler's opposition against pioneer powers, his tactical developments, and his political undertakings lastingly affect the aggregate memory of the Indian subcontinent. The imaginative utilization of rocket innovation, the moving partnerships in local governmental issues, and the conflict of societies during these struggles keep on being subjects of authentic examination and understanding.

Tipu Ruler's job as an image of obstruction against pilgrim powers has procured him esteem and debate in equivalent measure. His obligation to safeguarding Mysore's sway, his endeavors to produce partnerships against the English, and his tactical developments have made him a figure of verifiable importance. In any case, discusses encompassing his heritage persevere, with contrasting viewpoints on his arrangements, strict resilience, and the intricacies of his standard.

3.1 In-depth analysis of the Mysorean Wars against the British.

The Mysorean Wars, a progression of struggles that unfurled between the Realm of Mysore and the English East India Organization during the late eighteenth and mid nineteenth hundreds of years, comprise a critical part throughout the entire existence of pilgrim period India. The mind boggling elements of these conflicts, otherwise called the Old English Mysore Wars, mirror the intricacies of international connections, military techniques, and the conflict of two considerable powers in the Indian subcontinent.

The foundations of the Mysorean Wars can be followed back to the developing political scene of eighteenth century India. The decay of the Mughal Domain had made a power vacuum, inciting the rise of territorial powers competing for incomparability. Mysore, under the administration of Ruler Hyder Ali, arose as a critical player in the Deccan locale. The regional desires of the English East India Organization and the essential goals of Mysore set up for a progression of struggles that would shape the predetermination of the subcontinent.

The Primary Old English Mysore War (1767-1769) denoted the underlying showdown among Mysore and the English East India Organization. The conflict was established in regional debates and clashing financial interests. Ruler Hyder Ali, seeing the danger presented by the growing English impact, started military missions against the English. The contention finished up with the Deal of Madras in 1769, however the basic strains stayed unsettled, planting the seeds for future threats.

The command of Tipu Ruler to the privileged position of Mysore in 1782 denoted a basic crossroads and set up for the resulting clashes. Tipu Ruler, the Tiger of Mysore, acquired a realm confronting outside dangers and looked to shield Mysore's sway against the tireless expansionism of the English. The Second Old English Mysore War (1780-1784) unfurled against the background of moving collusions and international intricacies.

The tactical methodologies utilized by Tipu King during the Second Old English Mysore War displayed a mix of custom and development. The Clash of Pollilur in 1780 was a turning point, showing Tipu Ruler's tactical splendor and the powerful utilization of Mysorean rockets. The Mysoreans got a critical triumph against the English, underlining the inventive military techniques utilized by Tipu King. Regardless of strategic triumphs, the conflict closed with the Settlement of Mangalore in 1784, giving a brief end of threats.

The recess between the Second and Third Old English Mysore Wars was set apart by strategic moving, moving collusions, and the intricacies of territorial governmental issues. Tipu Ruler, perceiving the requirement for a unified front against the English, looked for coalitions with the Marathas and the Nizam. In any case, the liquid idea of unions in eighteenth century India implied that these organizations were many times fleeting, with interests wandering and combining in light of the international setting.

The Third Old English Mysore War (1790-1792) saw restored threats among Mysore and the English East India Organization. Tipu Ruler, confronting an imposing English reaction, attempted to keep up with the unions with the Marathas and the Nizam. The contention brought about the Deal of Seringapatam in 1792, forcing critical regional and monetary concessions on Mysore. The deficiency of key districts denoted a difficulty for Tipu Ruler and set up for the last a showdown in the Mysorean Wars.

The Fourth Old English Mysore War (1798-1799) unfurled against the background of increased strains and Tipu Ruler's proceeded with opposition against pioneer powers. The international real factors, combined with the English East India Organization's assurance to curb the Tiger of Mysore, prompted the attack of Srirangapatna in 1799. The fall of the capital denoted the finish of Tipu King's standard and his demise on the war zone.

The tactical methodologies utilized by Tipu Ruler during the Mysorean Wars were portrayed by a powerful mix of custom and development. The imaginative utilization of rocket innovation, especially the celebrated Mysorean rockets, became meaningful of Tipu King's tactical ability. These rockets, with their high level plan and flexibility, exhibited a takeoff from ordinary techniques for fighting. The Skirmish of Pollilur in 1780, where the Mysoreans got a critical triumph against the English, featured the effect of this capricious weaponry.

Tipu Ruler's tactical insight reached out past rocketry to the association and preparing of his military. The Fauj-I-Khas, Tipu Ruler's military, went through thorough preparation, and its officers were furnished with normalized weapons. The professionalization of the military reflected Tipu Ruler's obligation to military greatness and his comprehension of the changing elements of fighting in the eighteenth hundred years.

Decisively, Tipu King embraced a proactive way to deal with defending Mysore's sway. The collusions with territorial powers, like the Marathas and the Nizam, pointed toward making a unified front against the English. The Settlement of Gajendragad in 1787 formalized the partnership between Mysore, the Marathas, and the Nizam, representing Tipu Ruler's endeavors to manufacture a local offset to pioneer powers.

The conciliatory elements of the Mysorean Wars added one more layer of intricacy to the contentions. Tipu Ruler's commitment with adjoining states, like the Marathas and the Nizam, mirrored the perplexing trap of partnerships and contentions in eighteenth century India. The Settlement of Gajendragad, while representing a unified front against the English, likewise featured the difficulties of supporting collusions despite moving international elements.

Tipu Ruler's relations with the English East India Organization were key to the Mysorean Wars. The English, driven by royal desires and financial interests, looked to grow their impact in the Indian subcontinent. Tipu King's opposition against frontier powers displayed his assurance to protect Mysore's independence. The Settlement of Mangalore in 1784 and the Arrangement of Seringapatam in 1792 gave brief reprieves yet didn't determine the basic strains.

The Fourth Old English Mysore War, finishing in the attack of Srirangapatna, denoted the finish of Tipu King's standard and the proper extension of Mysore by the English East India Organization. The international scene of the Indian subcontinent went through a critical change, with the pilgrim power merging its impact over huge regions.

The tradition of the Mysorean Wars reaches out past the verifiable story of the contentions. Tipu Ruler's opposition against provincial powers, his tactical developments, and his strategic undertakings lastingly affect the aggregate memory of the Indian subcontinent. The imaginative utilization of rocket innovation, the moving coalitions in provincial legislative issues, and the conflict of societies during these struggles keep on being subjects of authentic examination and translation.

The Mysorean Wars are a demonstration of the complicated exchange of military procedures, strategic suggestions, and the conflict of provincial and pioneer powers in eighteenth century India. The tradition of Tipu Ruler, as an image of obstruction against pilgrim powers, stays a subject of profound respect and debate. His obligation to shielding Mysore's sway, his endeavors to manufacture unions against the English, and his tactical developments have made him a figure of verifiable importance.

3.2 Key battles and military campaigns led by Tipu Sultan.

Tipu Ruler, the Tiger of Mysore, scratched his name in history through a progression of key fights and military missions that characterized his rule during the late eighteenth hundred years.

His essential splendor, imaginative military strategies, and relentless assurance were exhibited in these urgent minutes that unfurled against the background of the Somewhat English Mysore Wars, denoting the unique cooperation among Mysore and the English East India Organization.

The Clash of Pollilur in 1780 stands as a demonstration of Tipu Ruler's tactical keenness and the imaginative utilization of rocket innovation. This fight, part of the Second Somewhat English Mysore War, unfurled nearby Pollilur, an essential area in the Deccan district. Tipu King, confronting the English powers drove by Sir Hector Munro, contrived a strategic masterstroke that would turn into a vital crossroads in his tactical missions.

The creative utilization of Mysorean rockets, frequently alluded to as "Tipu's Rockets," became meaningful of Tipu King's tactical ability. These rockets, with their high level plan and versatility, were conveyed actually on the war zone, surprising the English powers. The Mysorean rockets, furnished with iron cylinders and fueled by explosive, exhibited a degree of mechanical refinement that outperformed traditional big guns of the time. The Skirmish of Pollilur brought about a reverberating triumph for the Mysoreans, highlighting the viability of these unpredictable weapons.

Past the strategic splendor of the rocketry, Tipu King's essential situating and composed troop developments assumed a critical part in the accomplishment at Pollilur. The fight exhibited his capacity to coordinate customary Indian fighting strategies with inventive and current techniques, making an imposing power that could adjust to the changing elements of eighteenth century fighting.

The outcome of the Skirmish of Pollilur saw Tipu Ruler merging his tactical gains and chasing after a proactive methodology against the English. Notwithstanding, the intricacies of territorial partnerships and the liquid idea of international relations implied that the conflict would go on with its rhythmic movement.

The Third Somewhat English Mysore War (1790-1792) denoted one more critical stage in Tipu Ruler's tactical missions. Confronted with restored threats from the English, Tipu Ruler looked to shield Mysore against the imposing powers of the East India Organization. The contention saw a progression of commitment that tried the flexibility of Tipu Ruler's tactical procedures.

The Attack of Bangalore in 1791 was a vital second during the Third Somewhat English Mysore War. The English powers, drove by Broad Master Cornwallis, blockaded the essential city of Bangalore, a vital fortification for Tipu Ruler. The attack went on for a long time, featuring the relentlessness of the two sides. In any case, the competitive edge at last shifted for the English, and Bangalore fell into their hands.

The deficiency of Bangalore was a difficulty for Tipu King, however it didn't hose his soul of opposition. The ensuing commitment, including the Skirmish of Seedaseer and the Attack of Seringapatam, displayed Tipu Ruler's assurance to safeguard Mysore against overpowering chances. The many-sided strongholds of Seringapatam, Tipu King's capital, represented an imposing test for the English powers.

The Attack of Seringapatam in 1792, which finished up the Third Somewhat English Mysore War, denoted a defining moment in Tipu Ruler's tactical missions. The steady tension from the English, combined with the difficulties of supporting collusions with the Marathas and the Nizam, prompted the marking of the Deal of Seringapatam. The deal forced huge regional and monetary concessions on Mysore, flagging an impermanent end to threats.

The Fourth Somewhat English Mysore War (1798-1799) ended up being the last part in Tipu King's obstruction against the English. The international real factors, joined with Tipu King's proceeded with disobedience, set up for the unequivocal Attack of Srirangapatna in 1799. The English powers, drove by Broad Sir Arthur Wellesley, encompassed Tipu Ruler's capital, denoting the summit of an extended battle.

The Attack of Srirangapatna was a fierce and extreme commitment that unfurled inside the strengthened walls of the capital. Tipu Ruler, mindful of the imposing test, showed exceptional boldness and key intuition. The city, arranged on an island in the Cauvery Stream, introduced a characteristic protection, however the staggering could of the English powers in the long run penetrated the guards.

The fall of Srirangapatna in 1799 denoted the finish of Tipu King's standard and his passing on the combat zone. The English, victorious in their extension of Mysore, praised the triumph, yet the tradition of Tipu King persevered as an image of obstruction against provincial powers.

The critical fights and military missions drove by Tipu King offer a significant understanding into his dynamic way to deal with fighting. The Clash of Pollilur displayed his creative utilization of rocket innovation and his capacity to adjust to the changing idea of contention. The commitment during the Third Somewhat English Mysore War featured his versatility notwithstanding misfortune, with the Attack of Seringapatam filling in as an impactful snapshot of give up.

The Attack of Srirangapatna, while denoting the finish of Tipu King's obstruction, likewise cemented his inheritance as a bold protector of Mysore. The tactical missions drove by Tipu King, portrayed by a mix of custom and development, stay a subject of verifiable examination and deference. His obligation to shielding Mysore's sway against provincial powers and his creative military methodologies enduringly affect the authentic story of eighteenth century India.

As we ponder the critical fights and military missions drove by Tipu King, we are stood up to with a complicated and complex inheritance. Tipu King's job as a tactical leader, specialist, and image of opposition against frontier powers keeps on being a subject of verifiable request and translation. The powerful exchange of fighting, discretion, and advancement during these missions highlights the getting through meaning of Tipu King in the records of Indian history.

3.3 Examination of alliances and rivalries during this period.

The late eighteenth 100 years in India was portrayed by a complex international scene set apart by moving coalitions, provincial competitions, and the infringement of European pilgrim powers. Looking at the partnerships and contentions during this period gives a nuanced comprehension of the complex trap of connections that formed the fate of different states, especially against the background of the Old English Mysore Wars and the unmistakable job of Tipu Ruler.

One of the vital participants in this unpredictable dance of collusions was the Maratha Alliance. The Marathas, a strong Hindu fighter bunch, tried to declare strength over the Deccan district. Nonetheless, the Marathas were not a solid substance but rather a confederation of semi-independent states under the free control of the Chhatrapati. This inside intricacy made the Marathas both possible partners and adversaries for states like Mysore.

Tipu King, conscious of the provincial power elements, took part in strategic suggestions with the Marathas at different focuses during the Somewhat English Mysore Wars. The possibility of a unified front against normal enemies, particularly the English East India Organization, incited Tipu King to look for collusions with the Marathas. The Deal of Gajendragad in 1787 formalized such a partnership, mirroring an uncommon snapshot of territorial solidarity against pioneer powers.

In any case, the liquid idea of coalitions in eighteenth century India implied that associations were many times transient, with interests separating and uniting in light of the international setting. The Marathas, driven by their regional desires, had their own plan, and keeping a supported coalition demonstrated testing. The back and forth movement of Maratha-Mysore relations exhibited the sensitive equilibrium expected in exploring the unpredictable trap of partnerships during this period.

The Nizam of Hyderabad was one more huge player in the Deccan district, imparting lines to both the Marathas and Mysore. The Nizam's essential advantages once in a while lined up with those of Mysore, introducing potential open doors for joint effort, yet at different times, clashes emerged because of dissimilar desires.

The Nizam's arrangement with Mysore could give an impressive front against outer dangers, especially from the English. Alternately, the Nizam's advantages at times tangled with those of Mysore, prompting times of stressed relations and, surprisingly, military showdowns.

The Arrangement of Gajendragad in 1787, which formalized the coalition between Mysore, the Marathas, and the Nizam, exemplified the multifaceted dance of collusions during this period. The settlement pointed toward making a unified front against the English, mirroring an essential comprehension of the requirement for territorial participation. In any case, the life span of such collusions stayed questionable, given the dissimilar interests and the steadily changing elements of eighteenth century Indian legislative issues.

The Somewhat English Mysore Wars, traversing a very long while, brought the English East India Organization into direct struggle with Mysore and molded the unions and competitions of the period. The English, driven by financial interests and royal desires, looked to declare command over the Indian subcontinent. Mysore, under Tipu King, arose as a considerable snag to their arrangements.

The Primary Somewhat English Mysore War (1767-1769) set up for the extended clash among Mysore and the English East India Organization. The underlying threats were established in regional debates and clashing interests. Tipu Ruler's dad, King Hyder Ali, started military missions against the English, establishing the groundwork for Tipu Ruler's later showdowns.

The Settlement of Madras in 1769 closed the Main Old English Mysore War, yet it didn't determine the hidden strains. The international scene stayed full of rivalry, and Tipu King, after rising to the privileged position, confronted the impressive test of protecting Mysore against the constant expansionism of the English.

The Second Old English Mysore War (1780-1784) saw Tipu King's aggressive endeavors to fashion a unified front against the English. The coalitions with the Marathas and the Nizam, as epitomized in the Settlement of Gajendragad, looked to make a provincial offset to pioneer powers. The contention, set apart by the Clash of Pollilur and different commitment, exhibited Tipu Ruler's tactical keenness at the end of the day finished with the Arrangement of Mangalore in 1784.

The transitory suspension of threats gave a short rest, however the fundamental pressures continued. The resulting years saw Tipu Ruler participating in a fragile difficult exercise, exploring the intricacies of provincial governmental issues and outside dangers. The Deal of Mangalore, while offering a time of relative soundness, didn't check the finish of threats, as the English East India Organization kept on holding onto desires of enslaving Mysore.

The Third Somewhat English Mysore War (1790-1792) unfurled against the scenery of restored threats among Mysore and the English. Tipu King's endeavors to oppose provincial powers were met with an imposing English reaction. The Deal of Seringapatam in 1792, which finished up the conflict, forced critical regional and monetary concessions on Mysore. The deficiency of domain, including significant posts and vital locales, denoted a misfortune for Tipu Ruler.

The Fourth Somewhat English Mysore War (1798-1799) ended up being the climax of the contention among Mysore and the English East India Organization. The international real factors, combined with Tipu King's obstruction against pilgrim powers, prompted the attack of Srirangapatna in 1799. The fall of the capital denoted the finish of Tipu King's standard and his demise on the war zone.

Tipu King's political undertakings were not exclusively bound to military collusions and clashes. His effort stretched out to other Muslim powers, mirroring a more extensive vision of container Islamic fortitude. His correspondence with the Ottoman Realm, endeavors to lay out attaches with the leaders of Afghanistan, and strategic suggestions to the French were grounded in a common Islamic personality that rose above provincial limits.

Nonetheless, these strategic drives confronted difficulties, and the international real factors of the time frequently confounded Tipu Ruler's endeavors to manufacture a strong dish Islamic front. The Ottoman Realm, while communicating fortitude, didn't offer the tactical help that Tipu King looked for. The moving collusions and clashing interests among Muslim powers reflected the intricacies of conciliatory relations in the eighteenth hundred years.

The assessment of coalitions and competitions during this period highlights the perplexing idea of eighteenth century Indian international affairs. The smoothness of collusions, driven by logical contemplations and key goals, implied that territorial powers needed to explore an intricate trap of connections. Tipu King, as a ruler definitely cognizant of these intricacies, participated in conciliatory suggestions with the Marathas, the Nizam, and other Muslim powers, perceiving the requirement for local collaboration against outside dangers.

The Somewhat English Mysore Battles, as a setting to these discretionary moves, mirrored the conflict between pioneer desires and local powers endeavoring to keep up with their independence. The coalitions framed and disintegrated during these conflicts exemplified the difficulties of supporting helpful endeavors in a scene set apart by disparate interests and moving devotions.

Chapter 4

The Administration of Mysore

The organization of Mysore during the late eighteenth hundred years, subject to Tipu Ruler, was set apart by a special mix of military strength, financial strategies, and inventive administration. Tipu Ruler, frequently alluded to as the Tiger of Mysore, acquired the privileged position in 1782 and confronted the imposing test of safeguarding his realm against outer dangers, especially from the English East India Organization. Inspecting the organization of Mysore during this period offers bits of knowledge into the political, monetary, and social elements that formed the state.

Political Design and Administration:

Tipu King's political construction was described by a brought together and dictator administration framework. As a tactical pioneer, Tipu King expected both political and military obligations, uniting power in his grasp. The authoritative contraption rotated around the Ruler, who went with key choices connected with administration, tact, and military systems.

The capital city of Srirangapatna filled in as the managerial focus of Mysore. The strengthened island city on the Cauvery Waterway turned into an image of Tipu Ruler's standard, and its essential area added to the safeguard of the realm. The organization was coordinated around the regal court, where key pastors and consultants assumed urgent parts in the dynamic cycle.

Tipu King's administration style drew motivation from his dad, Ruler Hyder Ali, who had carried out managerial changes during his standard. The framework consolidated components of the conventional Mysorean managerial construction while acquainting developments with address the difficulties of the time.

Monetary Approaches and Income Organization:

Monetary strategies under Tipu King pointed toward supporting the monetary strength of Mysore, fundamental for supporting military endeavors against outer enemies. The financial construction was fundamentally agrarian, with agribusiness framing the foundation of the realm's income. Tipu King executed measures to work on rural efficiency, including land changes and water system projects.

The state's income framework depended on the customary land income framework pervasive in the district. Land income, gathered in real money or kind, comprised a critical piece of the state's pay. Tipu Ruler, mindful of the monetary significance of horticulture, acquainted measures with give help to ranchers during seasons of pain, mirroring a realistic way to deal with administration.

Notwithstanding agrarian strategies, Tipu King zeroed in on modern and business exercises. He empowered exchange and business, looking to broaden the wellsprings of income. The foundation of state imposing business models on specific products, including salt and tobacco, was an eminent element of Tipu Ruler's monetary strategies. These restraining infrastructures pointed toward producing state income and guaranteeing command over key products.

The presentation of another money framework, highlighting engravings in Persian and Kannada, reflected Tipu Ruler's endeavors to attest Mysore's social and financial personality. The financial approaches were intently attached to the more extensive objective of accomplishing independence and diminishing reliance on outer powers.

Military Organization and Advancement:

Given the international difficulties Mysore confronted, military organization was a foundation of Tipu King's standard. The Fauj-I-Khas, Tipu Ruler's own military, was a thoroughly prepared and trained force that assumed a urgent part in the protection of Mysore. The tactical organization was coordinated progressively, with key administrators and officials liable for different units.

One of the outstanding parts of Tipu Ruler's tactical organization was the mix of mechanical development into fighting. The utilization of cutting edge weaponry, including the renowned Mysorean rockets, displayed Tipu King's obligation to modernizing the military. These rockets, with their prevalent reach and versatility, turned into an image of Mysore's tactical ability.

The foundation of munititions stockpiles for the creation and capacity of weapons exemplified Tipu Ruler's accentuation on military readiness. The state's command over the creation of arms and ammo guaranteed a consistent inventory for the military. The military-modern complex under Tipu Ruler's organization added to the realm's capacity to oppose outer animosity.

Strategy and Unfamiliar Relations:

Tipu Ruler's discretion was formed by the objectives of shielding Mysore's power despite outside dangers. His way to deal with unfamiliar relations was down to earth, and he looked for partnerships with local powers to make a unified front against the English East India Organization. The settlements with the Marathas and the Nizam, formalized in the Deal of Gajendragad in 1787, reflected Tipu Ruler's endeavors to construct an alliance against pilgrim powers.

Tipu King's discretionary undertakings stretched out past the Indian subcontinent. He kept up with correspondence with the Ottoman Domain, looking for help and fortitude from the more extensive Muslim world. While the Ottoman reaction missed the mark regarding huge military guide, the discretionary commitment highlighted Tipu King's endeavors to situate Mysore inside a bigger international setting.

Social and Strict Strategies:

Tipu Ruler's organization additionally left an engraving on the social and strict scene of Mysore. His support of artistic expression and advancement of the Persian language added to the social wealth of the realm. The imperial court turned into a focal point of abstract and social exercises, with writers and researchers tracking down help and support.

While Tipu Ruler himself was a passionate Muslim, his way to deal with strict strategies showed a level of resistance. He delegated people from different strict networks to managerial positions, and the state didn't separate in view of religion. Notwithstanding, verifiable records likewise note examples of constrained changes and the obliteration of sanctuaries during explicit military missions, mirroring the mind boggling transaction of strict elements during the period.

Foundation and Metropolitan Turn of events:

Metropolitan turn of events and foundation got consideration under Tipu King's organization. The capital city of Srirangapatna saw the development of strongholds, royal residences, and different designs. The island city, with its very much arranged format, mirrored an essential way to deal with metropolitan turn of events.

Tipu King's advantage in mechanical advancement reached out to structural designing undertakings. He attempted drives to further develop water system frameworks, zeroing in on channels and water the executives. These undertakings pointed toward improving horticultural efficiency and guaranteeing the prosperity of the populace.

The essential area of Srirangapatna, encompassed by the Cauvery Stream, added to its normal guard. The city's strongholds were reinforced, and the generally speaking metropolitan arranging reflected contemplations of both military methodology and city improvement.

Inheritance and Authentic Viewpoints:

The organization of Mysore under Tipu King left an enduring effect on the verifiable story of the district. Tipu Ruler's obstruction against the English East India Organization, his tactical developments, and his endeavors to modernize administration have added to his heritage as an image of insubordination.

Verifiable viewpoints on Tipu Ruler's organization are assorted and frequently molded by contemporary political and social contemplations. While a few view him as a courageous safeguard of Mysore's sway and a benefactor of culture, others feature the intricacies of his standard, including occurrences of strict narrow mindedness and constrained changes.

4.1 Overview of Tipu Sultan's administrative reforms.

Tipu Ruler, the Tiger of Mysore, rose to the high position in 1782 and confronted the impressive test of safeguarding his realm against outside dangers, especially from the English East India Organization. His rule saw a progression of regulatory changes pointed toward reinforcing the state, modernizing administration, and guaranteeing the prosperity of the general population. An outline of Tipu Ruler's regulatory changes gives bits of knowledge into the multi-layered approach he embraced to explore the difficulties of the late eighteenth 100 years.

1. **Unified Administration:**

   One of the characterizing elements of Tipu King's managerial changes was the foundation of an incorporated administration framework. Drawing motivation from his dad, Ruler Hyder Ali, Tipu King solidified political and military expert in his grasp. The Ruler expected both political and military obligations, making a framework where key choices were made at the most elevated level of initiative.

   The regal court in Srirangapatna turned into the focal point of authoritative exercises. Key priests and counselors assumed critical parts in the dynamic cycle, however a definitive authority rested with Tipu Ruler. This brought together methodology considered quick direction, especially with regards to military techniques and strategic undertakings.

2. **Land Income Changes:**

   Farming framed the foundation of Mysore's economy during this period, and land income was a critical wellspring of state pay. Tipu King acquainted land income changes with upgrade horticultural efficiency and guarantee a consistent income stream for the state. His strategies pointed toward finding some kind of harmony between the monetary necessities of the state and the government assistance of the cultivating local area.

   Tipu Ruler executed a framework where land income was surveyed in light of the ripeness of the dirt and the idea of yields developed. The objective was to give help to ranchers during seasons of pain and to energize rural creation. Furthermore, he attempted measures to further develop water system frameworks, perceiving the basic job of water the board in supporting farming.

3. **Financial Broadening and State Syndications:**

   Tipu King's monetary approaches stretched out past horticulture to include exchange, industry, and business. Perceiving the significance of financial independence, he tried to enhance the wellsprings of state income. To accomplish this, Tipu Ruler carried out state imposing business models on specific products, including salt and tobacco.

   The foundation of state syndications permitted the public authority to control the creation, appropriation, and evaluating of key products. This produced income for the state as well as guaranteed a level of command over fundamental products. In any case, the execution of syndications was not without challenges, and authentic records feature occasions of opposition from impacted portions of society.

4. **Military Changes and Mechanical Development:**

   Given the international difficulties Mysore confronted, military changes were a focal part of Tipu King's organization. The Fauj-I-Khas, Tipu Ruler's own military, went through thorough preparation and discipline. The tactical organization was coordinated progressively, with key commandants and officials answerable for different units.

   One of the most remarkable parts of Tipu King's tactical changes was the joining of mechanical development into fighting. The utilization of cutting edge weaponry, especially the popular Mysorean rockets, exhibited his obligation to modernizing the military. The rockets, with their unrivaled reach and portability, became significant of Mysore's tactical ability during the Old English Mysore Wars.

   Notwithstanding rocketry, Tipu Ruler put resources into the development of arms and ammo through the foundation of munititions stockpiles. The state's command over the military-modern complex guaranteed a consistent stockpile of weapons for the military. These tactical advancements reflected Tipu King's essential premonition in planning Mysore for outer dangers.

5. **Discretionary Drives and Partnerships:**

   Discretion assumed an essential part in Tipu King's endeavors to shield Mysore's sway. Perceiving the requirement for a unified front against the English East India Organization, Tipu Ruler took part in political drives with territorial powers. The Deal of Gajendragad in 1787 formalized a partnership with the Marathas and the Nizam, mirroring an essential comprehension of the significance of local collaboration.

   Past the Indian subcontinent, Tipu Ruler's conciliatory undertakings reached out to the Ottoman Domain. His correspondence with the Ottoman rulers looked for help and fortitude from the more extensive Muslim world. While the Ottoman reaction didn't convert into critical military guide, the conciliatory commitment featured Tipu King's endeavors to situate Mysore inside a bigger international setting.

6. **Social and Instructive Support:**

   Tipu Ruler's organization likewise showed a distinct fascination with social and instructive support. The illustrious court in Srirangapatna turned into a focal point of abstract and social exercises, drawing in writers, researchers, and craftsmen. Tipu Ruler's help for the Persian language added to the social wealth of the realm.

   Instructive organizations got consideration, with the foundation of schools and universities. The objective was to advance learning and scholarly pursuits. The accentuation on social and instructive support reflected Tipu Ruler's more extensive vision of making a prospering and illuminated society inside Mysore.

7. **Foundation Advancement:**

Metropolitan turn of events and foundation got huge consideration under Tipu Ruler's organization. The capital city of Srirangapatna saw the development of fortresses, royal residences, and different designs. The invigorated island city filled in as an image of Mysore's solidarity and versatility.

Framework improvement stretched out past military contemplations to incorporate structural designing undertakings. Tipu Ruler started drives to further develop water system frameworks, zeroing in on trenches and water the executives. These undertakings pointed toward upgrading agrarian efficiency and guaranteeing the prosperity of the populace.

8. **Strict Arrangements and Resilience:**

Tipu King's strict strategies mirrored a level of resilience, regardless of cases of strict discussion during explicit military missions. His organization named people from different strict networks to managerial positions, and the state didn't segregate in light of religion.

Be that as it may, authentic records additionally note cases of constrained transformations and the annihilation of sanctuaries during explicit military missions. These activities, found with regards to the mind boggling strict elements of the time, remain points of authentic discussion and understanding.

Heritage and Verifiable Viewpoints:

The regulatory changes of Tipu Ruler left an enduring effect on the verifiable story of Mysore. His endeavors to modernize administration, fortify the economy, and guard against outer dangers have added to his heritage as an image of resistance against pilgrim powers.

Verifiable points of view on Tipu King's regulatory changes are different and frequently formed by contemporary political and social contemplations. Some view him as a visionary chief who looked to modernize Mysore and oppose settler powers, while others feature the intricacies of his standard, including occurrences of strict narrow mindedness and constrained transformations.

4.2 Economic policies and trade initiatives.

Tipu Ruler's monetary arrangements and exchange drives during the late eighteenth century were indispensable parts of his more extensive methodology to sustain the financial underpinning of Mysore and guarantee its strength against outside pressures, especially from the English East India Organization. His rule saw a mix of agrarian changes, exchange broadening, and financial independence measures. An investigation of Tipu Ruler's monetary strategies and exchange drives gives experiences into his visionary way to deal with financial administration.

1. **Agrarian Changes and Rural Efficiency:**

   Farming assumed a urgent part in the monetary scene of Mysore, and Tipu Ruler perceived the need to improve horticultural efficiency. His agrarian changes pointed toward making a more proficient and impartial framework. The evaluation of land income depended on variables, for example, soil fruitfulness and the idea of yields developed, mirroring a nuanced comprehension of the horticultural scene.

   Tipu Ruler's arrangements tried to mitigate the weight on the cultivating local area during times of misery. Exceptional consideration was given to water system undertakings to guarantee ideal water the board, significant for supporting agrarian result. These actions pointed toward establishing a favorable climate for ranchers, adding to expanded yields and generally speaking monetary dependability.

2. **Monetary Expansion and State Imposing business models:**

   Tipu Ruler sought after monetary broadening as a way to lessen reliance on unambiguous areas and wellsprings of income. To accomplish this, he carried out state imposing business models on specific products, a striking model being salt and tobacco. The foundation of imposing business models permitted the state to manage the creation, circulation, and evaluating of these items.

   The reasoning behind state imposing business models was twofold. It, first and foremost, gave a controlled climate to monetary exercises, guaranteeing security and consistency. Besides, it created income for the state, adding to the monetary strength vital for military readiness. Be that as it may, the execution of imposing business models confronted opposition from fragments of society, highlighting the difficulties intrinsic in such financial mediations.

3. **Exchange Broadening and Business Drives:**

   Exchange broadening was a critical component of Tipu Ruler's monetary vision. He looked to extend Mysore's monetary skylines by empowering exchange with different areas. The state effectively participated in business exercises, and Tipu King advanced the improvement of exchange organizations and courses.

   The foundation of conciliatory and exchange relations with unfamiliar powers reflected Tipu King's worldwide viewpoint. He looked for coalitions past the Indian subcontinent, encouraging financial binds with the Ottoman Domain and investigating open doors for coordinated effort with European countries. These drives were driven by the craving to get elective roads for exchange and to situate Mysore as a functioning member in the worldwide financial scene.

4. **Money Changes and Social Character:**

   As a component of his monetary strategies, Tipu King presented money changes pointed toward stating Mysore's social and financial character. The new money framework highlighted engravings in Persian and Kannada, underlining a feeling of social pride and peculiarity. The coins bore the name of Tipu Ruler, further highlighting the ruler's job in forming the financial story of the realm.

The money changes likewise reflected Tipu Ruler's familiarity with the emblematic significance of cash in projecting state authority. By presenting a money framework lined up with Mysorean social character, he looked to support the financial power of the realm.

5. **Framework Improvement and Financial Flexibility:**

Framework improvement was a pivotal part of Tipu King's financial technique. The development of fortresses, royal residences, and different designs in the capital city of Srirangapatna added to metropolitan turn of events. The braced island city not just filled in as an image of military strength yet in addition assumed a part in monetary versatility by giving a safe regulatory and business center point.

Structural designing undertakings zeroed in on further developing water system frameworks, including trenches and water the board drives. These tasks pointed toward improving rural efficiency, a foundation of Mysore's financial security. The essential improvement of framework was lined up with the more extensive objective of guaranteeing the prosperity of the general population and strengthening the financial groundwork of the realm.

6. **Financial Independence and Versatility:**

Tipu King's financial arrangements were outfitted towards accomplishing independence, lessening reliance on outer sources, and building flexibility despite outside dangers. The accentuation on horticultural changes, exchange enhancement, and state command over key monetary exercises were completely pointed toward making a self-supporting financial model.

The idea of monetary strength reached out to military readiness. A monetarily powerful state, upheld by different monetary exercises, was better situated to finance and support an imposing military power. Tipu King's financial vision was unpredictably associated with his general objective of protecting Mysore against outer enemies.

7. **Difficulties and Reactions:**

While Tipu King's financial arrangements were driven by an essential vision, they were not without difficulties and reactions. The execution of state syndications confronted obstruction from those impacted by these monetary mediations. Pundits contended that such measures could smother rivalry and cutoff financial opportunity.

Also, the quest for monetary expansion and exchange drives confronted deterrents because of the international real factors of the time. The worldwide financial scene was set apart by contest among European powers, and getting great exchange relations required exploring complex strategic and business elements.

8. **Heritage and Authentic Viewpoints:**

Tipu Ruler's financial strategies and exchange drives passed on an enduring heritage that keeps on being a subject of verifiable investigation and translation. His accentuation on financial independence, agrarian changes, and exchange broadening mirrored a ground breaking way to deal with administration.

Authentic viewpoints on Tipu King's monetary strategies frequently line up with more extensive appraisals of his standard. Some view him as a visionary chief who looked to modernize Mysore's economy and invigorate the realm against outer tensions. Others underscore the difficulties and reactions, especially with regards to financial mediations that confronted opposition.

4.3 Social and cultural advancements under Tipu's rule.

Tipu King's standard during the late eighteenth century denoted a time of huge social and social headways in the realm of Mysore. As the Tiger of Mysore, Tipu King tried to encourage a feeling of character and pride among his subjects while executing strategies that focused on social enhancement and cultural advancement. An investigation of the social and social headways subject to Tipu's authority gives experiences into his diverse way to deal with administration.

1. **Social Support and the Persian Language:**

   Tipu Ruler was a supporter of human expression and writing, adding to the social dynamic quality of Mysore. The imperial court in Srirangapatna turned into a middle for writers, researchers, and craftsmen. Tipu Ruler's help for the Persian language was especially remarkable. Persian, as a language of organization and culture, was effectively advanced, mirroring the ruler's appreciation for its scholarly and verifiable importance.

   The development of Persian verse and writing thrived under Tipu Ruler's support. Artists and researchers tracked down consolation at the regal court, and their works added to the scholarly wealth of the realm. The advancement of Persian culture was important for Tipu Ruler's more extensive endeavors to shape a particular social character for Mysore.

2. **Compositional Support and Metropolitan Turn of events:**

   Metropolitan turn of events and compositional support were key parts of Tipu Ruler's endeavors to improve the social scene of Mysore. The capital city of Srirangapatna saw the development of fortresses, royal residences, and different designs. These design attempts were vital as far as fortresses as well as added to the stylish and social allure of the city.

   The sustained island city, encompassed by the Cauvery Stream, turned into an image of Tipu King's standard. The essential area and very much arranged format of Srirangapatna reflected contemplations of both military methodology and city advancement. Metropolitan preparation and engineering support under Tipu King's standard exhibited a promise to making an unmistakable and strong capital.

3. **Instructive Drives and Scholarly Pursuits:**

Tipu Ruler's rule saw an emphasis on instructive drives pointed toward advancing scholarly pursuits and learning. Schools and universities were laid out, mirroring a promise to instruction for the purpose of cultural headway. The ruler perceived the significance of developing a learned and illuminated people.

The illustrious court filled in as a center point for scholarly trade, drawing in researchers from different disciplines. The support of scholarly pursuits, combined with the support of Persian writing, added to the scholarly extravagance of Mysore during this period. Instructive drives under Tipu King's standard mirrored a more extensive vision of cultural advancement and social turn of events.

4. **Strict Arrangements and Resistance:**

Tipu King's way to deal with strict strategies showed a level of resilience, in spite of the fact that it was not without debate. He named people from different strict networks to managerial positions, mirroring a guarantee to inclusivity. The state didn't segregate in light of religion, and people were considered for their capacities as opposed to their strict affiliations.

Be that as it may, verifiable records additionally note cases of strict discussion during explicit military missions. The annihilation of sanctuaries and the constrained transformations of specific networks have been subjects of authentic discussion and understanding. The intricacies of Tipu Ruler's strict approaches feature the fragile equilibrium expected in exploring the different strict scene of his realm.

5. **Mechanical Development and Military Headways:**

While principally connected with military developments, mechanical headways during Tipu King's standard likewise had social and social ramifications. The well known Mysorean rockets, created under his initiative, displayed the innovative ability of Mysore. These rockets, with their predominant reach and versatility, added to military strength as well as became emblematic of mechanical advancement.

The military-modern complex laid out by Tipu Ruler, including munitions stockpiles for the creation and capacity of weapons, addressed a combination of innovation, industry, and military procedure. The headways in weaponry and military innovation extraordinarily affected the cultural and social story of Mysore, extending a picture of a realm at the cutting edge of mechanical advancement.

6. **Dish Islamic Fortitude and Discretion:**

Tipu King's discretionary drives reached out past the Indian subcontinent to incorporate endeavors to manufacture container Islamic fortitude.

His correspondence with the Ottoman Realm, looking for help and fortitude from the more extensive Muslim world, exemplified his vision of a unified front against outer dangers. While the Ottoman reaction didn't convert into critical military guide, the conciliatory commitment highlighted Tipu King's endeavors to situate Mysore inside a bigger international setting.

The quest for dish Islamic fortitude was grounded in a common Islamic character that rose above territorial limits. Tipu Ruler's political undertakings mirrored a comprehension of the interconnectedness of Islamic people group and a craving to use this solidarity to help Mysore.

7. **Monetary Approaches and Social Government assistance:**

The monetary approaches carried out by Tipu King had social repercussions, especially as far as friendly government assistance and the prosperity of the general population. Agrarian changes pointed toward upgrading horticultural efficiency were intended to help the cultivating local area. The evaluation of land income in view of variables, for example, soil fruitfulness and harvest nature mirrored a worry for the monetary government assistance of the horticultural area.

Moreover, financial enhancement and state command over specific products, like salt and tobacco, had suggestions for social government assistance. While state imposing business models confronted opposition, their execution pointed toward guaranteeing a consistent stock of fundamental products and creating income for social and military projects.

8. **Inheritance and Verifiable Points of view:**

Tipu King's social and social headways during his standard passed on an enduring inheritance that keeps on being a subject of verifiable request and understanding. His endeavors to shape a particular social personality for Mysore, combined with drives in schooling, engineering, and scholarly pursuits, added to a time of social dynamic quality.

Authentic points of view on Tipu King's social and social progressions are different and frequently molded by contemporary political and social contemplations. Some view him as a visionary chief who tried to advance social extravagance and scholarly turn of events, while others underscore the intricacies of his standard, including occurrences of strict contention and constrained transformations.

Chapter 5

The Fall of Seringapatam

The fall of Seringapatam, a crucial occasion in the late eighteenth 100 years, denoted the climax of the Old English Mysore Wars and had broad ramifications for the political scene of South India. The fall of this strengthened city, arranged on an island in the Cauvery Waterway, was entwined with the tactical methodologies, conciliatory moves, and moving coalitions that portrayed the mind boggling collaborations between the English East India Organization and the realm of Mysore, managed by Tipu King.

Foundation and Setting:

The international scene of South India in the late eighteenth century was characterized by epic showdowns, moving collusions, and regional desires. The English East India Organization, trying to extend its impact, experienced impressive obstruction from the realm of Mysore, drove by Tipu Ruler, otherwise called the Tiger of Mysore. The Somewhat English Mysore Wars, a progression of struggles between the two powers, set up for the possible fall of Seringapatam.

The contention between the English and Tipu King was energized by regional debates, monetary interests, and international contemplations. Tipu Ruler, mindful of the infringing danger presented by the English, tried to assemble coalitions with local powers and oppose the expansionist plan of the East India Organization. The elements of this international chessboard set the scenery for the climactic occasions prompting the fall of Seringapatam.

Military Systems and Fortresses:

The tactical systems utilized by Tipu Ruler and the English assumed a conclusive part in the destiny of Seringapatam. The braced island city was a considerable fortress, encompassed by the Cauvery Waterway and safeguarded by hearty strongholds. Tipu Ruler, perceiving the essential meaning of Seringapatam, put resources into its protections, making it an impressive deterrent for any future intruder.

The Mysorean rockets, a mechanical development presented by Tipu Ruler, added another aspect to the city's protections. These rockets, with their unrivaled reach and portability, became significant of Mysore's tactical ability. The military-modern complex laid out by Tipu Ruler, including munititions stockpiles for the creation and capacity of weapons, added to the city's capacity to endure attacks.

On the English side, military authorities like General Richard Wellesley (later Duke of Wellington) and General George Harris assumed critical parts in concocting methodologies to break the protections of Seringapatam. The English East India Organization, having gained from past experiences, adjusted its tactical strategies to go up against the difficulties presented by the very much braced city.

Tact and Moving Coalitions:

Tact and the elements of moving coalitions were basic to the occasions prompting the fall of Seringapatam. Tipu King, perceiving the requirement for a unified front against the English, participated in strategic drives with local powers. The Settlement of Gajendragad in 1787 formalized a union with the Marathas and the Nizam, making an alliance against provincial powers.

Nonetheless, the liquid idea of partnerships in the eighteenth century Indian subcontinent implied that loyalties could change in light of moving international contemplations. The Marathas, when partners of Tipu Ruler, went into discussions with the English, changing the overall influence in the area. This moving conciliatory scene had suggestions for the destiny of Seringapatam.

Key Missions and Fights:

The way to the fall of Seringapatam was cleared with key missions and fights that unfurled during the Somewhat English Mysore Wars. The Third Somewhat English Mysore War (1790-1792) saw critical military commitment, including the Skirmish of Pollilur and the Attack of Bangalore. These missions set up for the later contentions that would decide the destiny of Seringapatam.

The Fourth Old English Mysore War (1798-1799) was an unequivocal stage in the battle between the English and Tipu King. The Skirmish of Seringapatam in 1799, battled between the English powers under Broad Harris and Tipu Ruler's military, was the climactic showdown that would decide the fate of the strengthened city. The English, with their adjusted military systems and supported by Maratha and Nizam contingents, tried to penetrate the protections of Seringapatam.

The Attack of Seringapatam:

The Attack of Seringapatam, an extended and extreme military mission, unfurled in 1799 and denoted the last part in the battle for the city. The English powers, outfitted with cutting edge mounted guns and supported by their unions, blockaded the invigorated island. The geology of Seringapatam, encompassed by the Cauvery Waterway, represented a considerable test for the aggressors.

The attack was described by extreme siege and conflicts as the two sides took part in a battle for matchless quality. The Mysorean rockets, when an image of Tipu Ruler's tactical strength, were currently met with the capability of the English mounted guns. The mechanical deviation shifted the equilibrium for the aggressors.

The strategies utilized during the attack displayed the versatility of the English powers. Approaches, for example, building batteries and penetrating walls showed an essential comprehension of the difficulties presented by the city's strongholds. The extended idea of the attack negatively affected the two sides, with setbacks mounting and assets diminishing.

The Fall of Seringapatam:

The defining moment came the evening of May 4, 1799, when a break was effectively made in the walls of Seringapatam. The English powers, immediately jumping all over the chance, sent off a conclusive attack. Savage hand-to-hand battle resulted as English soldiers, alongside their Maratha and Nizam partners, battled their direction into the core of the city.

Amidst the mayhem, Tipu King, driving the guard of Seringapatam, met his shocking end. Verifiable records portray his courageous obstruction as he battled to the last minutes, epitomizing the soul of insubordination that described his standard. The fall of Tipu Ruler denoted the emblematic finish of Mysore's opposition against English expansionism.

The consequence of the fall of Seringapatam saw the city being pillaged, and tremendous changes were organized by the English in the political organization of the district. The English East India Organization arose as the prevailing power in South India, hardening its command over Mysore and modifying the international scene of the subcontinent.

Outcomes and Authentic Points of view:

The fall of Seringapatam had significant ramifications for the locale and for Tipu King's inheritance. The extension of Mysore by the English denoted the conclusion of a significant time period and the start of another stage throughout the entire existence of South India. The international realignment coming about because of the fall of Seringapatam reshaped partnerships and power elements in the area.

Verifiable viewpoints on the fall of Seringapatam differ, reflecting assorted stories and translations. Tipu Ruler, recognized as a brave safeguard of Mysore, turned into an image of obstruction against pilgrim powers. His sad end at Seringapatam added a layer of suffering to his heritage, adding to his getting through picture as the Tiger of Mysore.

For the English, the fall of Seringapatam addressed a huge military victory and built up their predominance in South India. The crown jewels of war, including Tipu Ruler's belongings and the abundance of the city, further advanced the English East India Organization. Nonetheless, the triumph likewise energized discussions and conversations in England with respect to the morals of domain building and the strategies utilized in accomplishing magnificent objectives.

5.1 Detailed account of the Siege of Seringapatam.

The Attack of Seringapatam in 1799 stands as a significant and emotional episode throughout the entire existence of South India, denoting the finish of the Fourth Old English Mysore War and a definitive destruction of Tipu King, the Tiger of Mysore. This definite record dives into the complexities of the attack, inspecting the tactical techniques, the geographic difficulties, the steady encounters, and the awful peak that unfurled inside the strengthened walls of Seringapatam.

Setting and Vital Importance:

The essential meaning of Seringapatam, arranged on an island in the Cauvery Waterway, was surely known by both the English East India Organization and Tipu Ruler. The city's considerable strongholds, combined with the regular obstruction of the stream, introduced a difficult snag for any eventual trespasser. As the capital of Mysore and an image of Tipu King's power, Seringapatam was the essential objective for the English in their endeavors to state strength in the locale.

The international scene paving the way to the attack was described by moving partnerships and the liquid elements of eighteenth century Indian legislative issues. Tipu Ruler, mindful of the infringing danger presented by the English, had looked for partnerships with local abilities, including the Marathas and the Nizam, to shape a unified front against pioneer powers. In any case, the elements of these unions were flighty, and the Marathas, when partners of Tipu Ruler, in the long run went into dealings with the English, changing the overall influence.

Readiness and Strongholds:

The groundwork for the attack of Seringapatam involved fastidious preparation and key contemplations with respect to the English powers. General George Harris, who drove the English campaign, perceived the requirement for adjusting military strategies to stand up to the difficulties presented by the very much strengthened city. The English powers were built up by contingents from the Marathas and the Nizam, denoting a change in the international scene.

Seringapatam's strongholds were a demonstration of Tipu Ruler's tactical sharpness. The city was enclosed areas of strength for by and strongholds, with the Cauvery Waterway filling in as a characteristic canal on one side. The considerable guards likewise incorporated an arrangement of external and inward fortresses, making any immediate attack an overwhelming undertaking. Tipu King, mindful of the essential weakness of the island, had put resources into its safeguards, including the development of solid defenses and the establishment of cannons.

The Topography of Seringapatam:

The geographic design of Seringapatam presented the two benefits and difficulties for the attacking powers. The island city, encompassed by the Cauvery Waterway, made a characteristic hindrance that restricted possible roads of assault. The waterway, while filling in as a protective element, likewise presented calculated difficulties for the English powers trying to lay out an attack.

The English, adjusting to the geographic imperatives, conceived procedures to defeat the regular obstructions. The presence of water bodies required the development of improvised spans, and the coordinated factors of getting cannons and troops across the stream added a layer of intricacy to the attack tasks. The geology of Seringapatam, while adding to its protections, required creative methodologies with respect to the blockading powers.

The Initiation of the Attack:

The conventional beginning of the attack happened in February 1799, as the English powers, alongside their Maratha and Nizam partners, started their enclosure of Seringapatam. The underlying phases of the attack included laying out positions and settlements, laying the foundation for the resulting periods of the activity. The operations of shipping troops, mounted guns, and supplies across the stream required cautious coordination.

The English powers, mindful of the difficulties presented by Seringapatam's fortresses, started an orderly way to deal with debilitate the guards. Ordnance assault designated the walls and strongholds, with the target of making breaks through which the going after powers could infiltrate. The clamor of cannons and the smoke of gunfire consumed the space as the besiegers and safeguards took part in a tenacious trade.

The Mysorean Rockets and Innovative Fighting:

A prominent part of the attack was the utilization of Mysorean rockets, a mechanical development presented by Tipu Ruler. These rockets, known for their unrivaled reach and versatility, had become significant of Mysore's tactical ability. The Mysorean rockets were terminated from launchers known as "rocket men," adding another aspect to the war zone and testing the customary techniques for fighting.

The English powers, experiencing the Mysorean rockets, needed to adjust to this mechanical imbalance. The rockets, with their capricious directions and wrecking influence, represented a danger to the two soldiers and ordnance. The English reaction included sending rockets of their own and creating countermeasures to alleviate the adequacy of Mysorean rocket assaults.

Extended Siege and Engagements:

The attack unfurled as an extended issue, with the English powers strengthening their barrage of Seringapatam's fortresses. The determined big guns blast expected to make breaks in the walls, considering an immediate attack on the city. The shielding powers, under the order of Tipu Ruler, answered sincerely, fixing breaks and repulsing assaults.

The encounters during the attack included close-quarter battle, as English and Mysorean troops conflicted nearby the breaks. The guards of Seringapatam, however exposed to huge tension, held firm during the beginning phases of the attack. The island city turned into a landmark, with the destiny of Mysore yet to be determined.

The Night Attack and Penetrating the Walls:

The defining moment in the attack came the evening of May 4, 1799, when an essential break was effectively made in the walls of Seringapatam. The English powers, immediately jumping all over the chance, sent off a conclusive night attack. Wild hand-to-hand battle resulted as the besiegers battled their direction through the break, confronting decided opposition from Tipu Ruler's powers.

The break in the walls denoted a basic crossroads in the attack, as the English powers, upheld by their Maratha and Nizam partners, entered the core of the city. The safeguards, however brave in their endeavors, were currently confronted with a mind-boggling force that had penetrated the once-secure fortresses. The roads of Seringapatam turned into a landmark, with the destiny of the city yet to be determined.

Fall of Tipu King:

In the disorder of the night attack, Tipu Ruler, driving the protection of Seringapatam, met his unfortunate end. Authentic records depict his bold opposition as he battled to the last minutes, epitomizing the soul of rebellion that described his standard. The fall of Tipu King denoted the representative finish of Mysore's obstruction against English expansionism.

The passing of Tipu Ruler had significant ramifications for the destiny of Seringapatam. With the fall of the Tiger of Mysore, the safeguards confronted an authority vacuum, and the energy had moved conclusively for the blockading powers. The English, supported by their partners and filled by the craving for triumph, pushed forward in the last phases of the attack.

Loot and Result:

The fall of Seringapatam on May 4, 1799, was trailed by scenes of loot and disorder. The triumphant English powers, anxious to guarantee the crown jewels of war, stripped the city. The abundance amassed by Tipu Ruler, including his belongings and the fortunes of the city, fell under the control of the vanquishers. The repercussions of the attack saw a change of Seringapatam, as the English East India Organization set its command over Mysore.

The political result of the fall of Seringapatam involved the revamping of the organization of Mysore under English suzerainty. The addition of Mysore denoted the conclusion of a significant time period, adjusting the international scene of South India. The tradition of Tipu King persevered as an image of opposition against pilgrim powers, even notwithstanding rout.

Verifiable Points of view and Inheritance:

The verifiable points of view on the Attack of Seringapatam fluctuate, reflecting different accounts and understandings. For the English, the fall of Seringapatam addressed a huge military victory and built up their predominance in South India. The victory of the strengthened city added toward the East India Organization's regional acquisitions and hardened its status as a principal power in the district.

Interestingly, Tipu Ruler's heritage persevered as an image of fearless obstruction. His shocking end at Seringapatam added a layer of suffering to his picture, and he turned into a commended figure in the Indian patriot story. The insubordination showed by Tipu Ruler during the attack, combined with his endeavors to oppose frontier development, made a permanent imprint on the social and political legacy of the Indian subcontinent.

5.2 Events leading to Tipu Sultan's eventual defeat.

The occasions prompting Tipu King's possible loss were molded by a mind boggling interaction of military contentions, political moves, moving coalitions, and key errors.

This story unfurls against the scenery of the late eighteenth hundred years, a period set apart by extreme international contentions and supreme desires in the Indian subcontinent.

1. **Somewhat English Mysore Wars and Early Struggles:**

   The seeds of Tipu Ruler's possible loss were planted with regards to the Somewhat English Mysore Wars, a progression of struggles between the English East India Organization and the Realm of Mysore. The Primary Old English Mysore War (1767-1769) saw beginning conflicts between the English and the powers of Hyder Ali, Tipu Ruler's dad. The Deal of Madras in 1769 finished the threats however set up for future showdowns.

   The Second Old English Mysore War (1780-1784) emitted because of heightening pressures and regional debates. Hyder Ali's passing in 1782 carried Tipu Ruler to the front of the contention. The English, drove by administrators like Lead representative General Warren Hastings and Lead representative General Ruler Cornwallis, confronted decided obstruction from Tipu King's powers. The conflict closed with the Settlement of Mangalore in 1784, reestablishing the norm prewar however leaving annoying issues that energized ensuing contentions.

2. **Strategic Moves and Partnerships:**

   Tipu King, perceiving the approaching danger presented by the English East India Organization, participated in political moves to protect unions with provincial powers. The Settlement of Gajendragad in 1787 formalized a partnership with the Marathas and the Nizam, making an alliance against the English. The discretionary scene was liquid, with partnerships moving in light of changing international contemplations.

   In any case, the intricacies of eighteenth century Indian governmental issues implied that unions were many times dubious and dependent upon sudden changes. The Marathas, when partners of Tipu Ruler, went into discussions with the English, changing the overall influence in the area. The moving elements of partnerships straightforwardly affected the occasions prompting Tipu Ruler's possible loss.

3. **Monetary Tensions and Exchange Strategies:**

   Monetary elements assumed an essential part in forming the occasions prompting Tipu King's loss. The financial arrangements sought after by Tipu Ruler, including state command over specific wares and the burden of syndications, confronted obstruction and made pressures inside his own realm. The endeavor to manage exchange, while driven by a craving for financial independence, had repercussions on the more extensive monetary scene.

The English East India Organization, with its growing financial interests, looked to get command over key shipping lanes and wares. The financial contest between the English and Mysore added a layer of intricacy to the international scene. Exchange approaches and monetary tensions became entwined with the more extensive military and political struggles, adding to the occasions prompting Tipu King's inevitable loss.

4. **Third Somewhat English Mysore War (1790-1792):**

The Third Somewhat English Mysore War denoted a basic stage in the occasions prompting Tipu Ruler's loss. The contention emitted in 1790, with Tipu Ruler trying to recover domains lost in past conflicts. The English, under the initiative of Lead representative General Cornwallis, answered with a restored assurance to check Mysorean power.

Key fights and commitment, including the Skirmish of Pollilur and the Attack of Bangalore, described the Third Old English Mysore War. The English, adjusting their tactical techniques, confronted imposing opposition from Tipu Ruler's powers. In any case, the tide changed with the catch of Bangalore and the resulting fights that debilitated Tipu Ruler's situation.

The Settlement of Seringapatam in 1792, which closed the Third Old English Mysore War, forced huge regional and financial concessions on Mysore. Tipu Ruler surrendered half of his realm to the English, paid a significant reimbursement, and consented to the terms that reduced his tactical capacities. The occasions of the Third Old English Mysore War denoted a misfortune for Tipu King and set up for the resulting clashes.

5. **Fourth Old English Mysore War (1798-1799):**

The Fourth Old English Mysore War, crossing 1798 to 1799, was the finish of the occasions prompting Tipu King's possible loss. The international scene had moved with the changing elements of partnerships, and the English, under Lead representative General Richard Wellesley, jumping all over the chance to control Tipu King's influence.

The conflict was set off by Tipu Ruler's hesitance to agree with the conditions of the Arrangement of Seringapatam completely. The English, deciphering this as a break of understanding, saw a potential chance to additionally debilitate Mysore. Tipu Ruler, mindful of the looming danger, tried to fabricate partnerships past the Indian subcontinent, participating in strategic drives with the Ottoman Domain and looking for dish Islamic fortitude.

6. **Key Fights and Military Missions:**

The Fourth Somewhat English Mysore War saw key fights and military missions that assumed an unequivocal part in the occasions prompting Tipu Ruler's loss. The Skirmish of Malavelly in 1799 saw conflicts among English and Mysorean powers. The English, with their predominant military systems and coalitions, acquired the advantage. The ensuing Attack of Seringapatam turned into the peak of the contention.

The English powers, built up by their Maratha and Nizam partners, participated in an extended attack of Seringapatam. The tactical techniques utilized during the attack, remembering big guns assault and the production of breaks for the walls, exhibited the versatility of the English powers. The fall of Seringapatam in May 1799 denoted the unfortunate finish of Tipu Ruler and the definitive loss of Mysore.

7. **The Fall of Seringapatam:**

The fall of Seringapatam in 1799 was the perfection of a progression of situation that had transpired over many years. The attack, described by serious siege, engagements, and a conclusive night attack, brought about the break of the city's fortresses. Tipu King, driving the protection, met his appalling end amidst wild hand-to-hand battle.

The outcomes of the fall of Seringapatam were significant. The city was ravaged by the triumphant English powers, and huge changes were established in the political organization of the district. The extension of Mysore denoted the conclusion of an important time period and set English command over South India.

8. **Heritage and Authentic Points of view:**

The occasions prompting Tipu Ruler's inevitable loss passed on an enduring inheritance that keeps on being a subject of verifiable examination and translation. Tipu King, recognized as the Tiger of Mysore and a brave safeguard against provincial powers, turned into an image of obstruction. His endeavors to fabricate coalitions, carry out monetary strategies, and participate in conciliatory drives mirrored a multi-layered way to deal with administration.

Authentic viewpoints on Tipu King's loss are different and frequently formed by contemporary political and social contemplations. Some view him as a visionary chief who looked to oppose pilgrim extension, while others underscore the intricacies of his standard, including disputable strategies and military missions.

5.3 Impact on the region and the end of the Fourth Anglo-Mysore War.

The effect of the Fourth Old English Mysore War and the fall of Seringapatam resounded all through the locale, denoting an extraordinary second in the political, social, and financial scene of South India. This period, coming full circle in 1799, saw the finish of Tipu King's standard and the combination of English authority in the Indian subcontinent. The situation that developed during and after the Fourth Old English Mysore War made a permanent imprint on the locale, molding its direction into the indefinite future.

1. **Extension of Mysore and Regional Realignments:**

The quick outcome of the Fourth Somewhat English Mysore War was the addition of the Realm of Mysore by the English East India Organization. With the fall of Seringapatam, the English attested command over the vital and financially huge area. The regions of Mysore were rearranged, and English authorities took command, supervising the administration of the recently gained domains.

The addition had significant ramifications for the political guide of South India. Mysore, when a strong and free realm, was presently retained into the growing English pilgrim domain. The regional realignments not just modified the international elements of the area yet additionally set up for additional English extension and solidification in the Indian subcontinent.

2. **The Arrangement of Seringapatam (1799):**

The finish of the Fourth Somewhat English Mysore War was formalized through the Deal of Seringapatam in 1799. This arrangement, haggled between the English and the delegates of Mysore, laid out the details of the political settlement. The arrangement depicted the circumstances under which Mysore would be directed under English suzerainty.

Key arrangements of the deal incorporated the disbandment of Tipu Ruler's military, the inconvenience of a reimbursement, and the cession of regions. The Nizam and the Marathas, who had aligned with the English during the conflict, were likewise allowed regional concessions. The deal set English strength in South India and made way for another period of pilgrim organization.

3. **Monetary Double-dealing and English Control:**

The extension of Mysore achieved huge changes in financial approaches and control. The English East India Organization, presently the true leader of Mysore, looked to take advantage of the financial assets of the district. Land income frameworks were rebuilt, and the presentation of new tax collection arrangements had broad ramifications for the agrarian economy.

The English executed monetary measures pointed toward augmenting income extraction. The abuse of normal assets, especially backwoods and mines, strengthened under pioneer rule. The monetary effect of English control was felt at different levels, influencing the agrarian and modern areas as well as the more extensive financial texture of the locale.

4. **Socio-Social Changes:**

The socio-social scene of the locale went through huge changes in the repercussions of the Fourth Somewhat English Mysore War. The extension of Mysore and the burden of English rule achieved changes in administration, organization, and social practices. English authorities assumed responsibility for authoritative issues, presenting new frameworks of equity, instruction, and administration.

Social support that had prospered under the Mysorean rule confronted moves and difficulties. The inconvenience of English standards and the foundation of pilgrim organizations affected social articulations. The elements of strict practices and social designs were additionally influenced, as the English looked to reshape specific parts of the socio-social texture to line up with frontier goals.

5. **Segment Changes and Settlements:**

The finish of the Fourth Somewhat English Mysore War saw segment changes because of English arrangements. The development of populaces, changes in landownership designs, and the foundation of new settlements added to segment shifts. The monetary approaches of the English, combined with agrarian changes, affected examples of land use and possession.

The foundation of English settlements and military cantonments further adjusted the segment scene. The convergence of English pilgrims, troopers, and directors presented another social dynamic, making areas of English impact inside the more extensive native populace. These segment changes were intelligent of the more extensive effect of pilgrim rule on the social construction of the area.

6. **English Military Presence and Fortresses:**

The English military presence in the repercussions of the conflict lastingly affected the locale's security and guard. The foundation of military cantonments and the development of strongholds became significant of English control. Vital areas were braced to get English interests and keep up with command over the recently obtained domains.

The tactical engineering presented by the English left a visual engraving on the scene. Fortifications and posts, decisively situated, represented the changelessness of English impact. These fortresses filled both protective and emblematic needs, underlining the tactical strength that went with provincial rule.

7. **Repercussions on Tipu King's Heritage:**

The loss of Tipu King and the finish of the Fourth Old English Mysore War had significant repercussions on the tradition of the Tiger of Mysore. Tipu King, recognized as a fearless safeguard against frontier powers, turned into an image of opposition and hostile to pilgrim feeling. The conditions of his passing throughout the fall of Seringapatam added a layer of suffering to his picture.

Tipu Ruler's heritage persevered as a mind boggling and multi-layered section throughout the entire existence of the Indian subcontinent. While some praised him as a public legend who remained against English colonialism, others studied specific parts of his standard, including his strict strategies and military missions. The discussion over Tipu Ruler's inheritance keeps on being a subject of verifiable talk and social stories.

8. **International Consequences:**

The international consequences of the Fourth Somewhat English Mysore War reached out past the limits of South India. The combination of English command over Mysore fortified the East India Organization's situation in the more extensive setting of royal competitions. The international scene of the Indian subcontinent was molded by the developing impact of the English, who arose as a fundamental power.

The extension of Mysore and the resulting international realignments had repercussions for local abilities and regal states. The essential overall influence moved, impacting discretionary relations and partnerships. The international scene set up for future contentions and discussions, adding to the developing elements of majestic governmental issues.

9. **Authentic Viewpoints and Challenged Stories:**

The occasions following the Fourth Somewhat English Mysore War are dependent upon different authentic points of view and challenged accounts. The effect of English pilgrim rule, while recognized for its groundbreaking impact, is in many cases broke down from alternate points of view. Some feature the financial and infrastructural advancements achieved by pioneer organization, while others underscore the shifty angles and socio-social interruptions.

The tradition of Tipu King stays a mark of verifiable conflict. Remembered as a legend in certain stories, Tipu King's commitments to the opposition against pioneer powers are commended. Nonetheless, varying viewpoints investigate specific arrangements and activities of his standard, starting discussions over the intricacy of his heritage.

10. **Long haul Ramifications for South India:**

The drawn out ramifications of the Fourth Old English Mysore War and the ensuing occasions formed the direction of South India in the nineteenth and twentieth hundreds of years. The locale turned into an indispensable piece of the English frontier organization, contributing financially and decisively to magnificent targets. The effect on administration, economy, and society established the groundwork for the development of a cutting edge South India inside the shapes of English India.

The traditions of pilgrim rule, including regulatory designs, overall sets of laws, and financial approaches, got through even after India acquired autonomy in 1947. The reverberations of the occasions following the Fourth Somewhat English Mysore War kept on resounding in the political, social, and social texture of South India.

Chapter 6

Legacy in Warfare

The tradition of Tipu King in fighting is well established in his essential sharpness, military developments, and a persevering obligation to oppose frontier powers during a wild period in Indian history. The Tiger of Mysore, as Tipu Ruler is frequently alluded to, made a permanent imprint on the craft of war, forming the tradition of Mysorean military procedures and advancements that affected ensuing ages.

1. **Imaginative Military Systems:**
   Tipu Ruler, acquiring the tactical ability of his dad Hyder Ali, showed a sharp comprehension of imaginative military systems. His way to deal with fighting was described by a mix of ordinary and capricious strategies, showing an essential adaptability that put him aside. One of Tipu Ruler's remarkable commitments was the successful utilization of close quarters combat, a strategy that demonstrated important in opposing the thoroughly prepared and restrained English powers.

   Hit and run combat permitted Tipu King to take advantage of the geology of the Mysorean scene, using the thick timberlands and troublesome landscapes for his potential benefit. This eccentric procedure disturbed the conventional European military strategies utilized by the English, making a critical test for their officers. Tipu King's capacity to adjust and improve notwithstanding a mechanically unrivaled enemy stamped him as a tactical tactician of excellent type.

2. **Mysorean Rockets:**
   Among the most famous advancements credited to Tipu King is the turn of events and sending of Mysorean rockets. These rockets, known for their long-reach and exactness, changed the front line during the late eighteenth 100 years. Tipu King perceived the capability of these rockets as an impressive weapon, and under his support, Mysore turned into a middle for the creation

and refinement of these tactical innovations.

The Mysorean rockets, frequently alluded to as "Mysore rockets" or "congrieve rockets," were utilized broadly in fights against the English. They offered a critical mechanical benefit, making frenzy and tumult among foe powers. The viability of these rockets turned into an image of Mysore's tactical ability and a demonstration of Tipu Ruler's obligation to mechanical development in fighting.

3. **Tiger of Mysore and Emblematic Fighting:**

   Tipu Ruler's tactical inheritance stretches out past the strategic and mechanical viewpoints to envelop emblematic fighting. The title "Tiger of Mysore" itself mirrors the picture he developed - one of a bold and decided pioneer. Tipu King decisively utilized images and symbols related with tigers in his tactical formal attire, banners, and seals, making a strong and suggestive visual character.

   This emblematic fighting had mental ramifications on the front line. The symbolism of the tiger, known for its solidarity and spryness, ingrained a feeling of satisfaction and courage among Tipu Ruler's soldiers. It likewise filled in as an image of opposition against unfamiliar mastery, revitalizing the Mysorean powers around a common character and reason. The Tiger of Mysore, both in substance and image, turned into a focal figure in the opposition against English expansionism.

4. **Tact and Coalitions:**

   Tipu King's heritage in fighting likewise incorporates his discretionary endeavors to manufacture unions against the English East India Organization. Perceiving the international intricacies of the time, Tipu Ruler participated in strategic moves to assemble alliances with territorial powers. The Settlement of Gajendragad in 1787, which formalized a partnership with the Marathas and the Nizam, embodies Tipu Ruler's conciliatory drives.

   While not generally fruitful in keeping up with stable coalitions, Tipu Ruler's strategic endeavors displayed a nuanced comprehension of the international scene. These coalitions, in any event, when brief, had key ramifications for the tactical missions against the English. The discretionary element of Tipu King's inheritance features his multi-layered way to deal with opposing provincial powers.

5. **Strongholds and Cautious Fighting:**

   Tipu King's tactical heritage is likewise apparent in the strongholds and guarded structures he raised to shield Mysore against outer dangers. Seringapatam, his capital, was a perfect representation of key strongholds. The island city on the Cauvery Waterway was encircled areas of strength for by, strongholds, and bulwarks, making it a considerable fort.

   The cautious fighting techniques executed by Tipu Ruler, particularly during the Old English Mysore Wars, showed a careful way to deal with safeguarding key regions. The development of posts, including those at Palakkad and Nandidurg, displayed his obligation to making protective borders that could endure delayed attacks. These strongholds reflected military contemplations as well as the more extensive international objectives of the time.

6. **Maritime Fighting and the Mysorean Naval force:**

Tipu Ruler's inheritance in fighting reached out to maritime commitment, a space where he tried to challenge English maritime predominance. The improvement of the Mysorean Naval force subject to his authority denoted an endeavor to counter English maritime power along the western shoreline of India. Tipu Ruler perceived the essential significance of a solid naval force in shielding his realm's seaside domains.

The Mysorean Naval force, furnished with cutting edge warships and advancements, took part in oceanic contentions against the English. In any case, the maritime undertakings confronted difficulties, and the English Illustrious Naval force kept up with its predominance in the waters. Regardless of limits, Tipu Ruler's endeavors to construct a maritime power mirrored his extensive way to deal with military systems, enveloping both land and ocean.

7. **Tradition of Opposition and Freedom:**

The general tradition of Tipu Ruler in fighting is that of a strong and decided pioneer who savagely opposed frontier infringement. Tipu King's obligation to the reason for autonomy and his steady endeavors to safeguard the power of Mysore left a getting through engrave on the historical backdrop of the Indian subcontinent. His tactical missions, set apart by snapshots of win and difficulties, epitomize the soul of opposition against majestic powers.

The Tiger of Mysore turned into an image of resistance, rousing people in the future in their battles for freedom. Tipu King's heritage, both regarding military procedures and the ethos of opposition, added to the more extensive account of against frontier developments in India. The memory of his bold endeavors continued as a wellspring of motivation during the later eases of the Indian freedom development in the twentieth 100 years.

8. **Verifiable Points of view and Contentions:**

The evaluation of Tipu King's heritage in fighting isn't without contentions and changing authentic viewpoints. While many view him as a chivalrous figure who remained against pioneer hostility, others investigate specific parts of his standard, including the treatment of non-Muslims and the direct of military missions. Authentic discussions over Tipu King's heritage mirror the intricacies of his standard and the assorted encounters of various networks during that period.

The discussion encompassing Tipu King's heritage acquired unmistakable quality in present day India, with contrasting understandings in view of provincial, strict, and political affiliations. The discussions highlight the significance of basically looking at verifiable accounts and perceiving the subtleties of Tipu Ruler's multi-layered heritage in fighting and administration.

6.1 Examination of Tipu Sultan's military strategies and innovations.

Tipu Ruler, the Tiger of Mysore, remains as a fascinating figure in the records of military history, famous for his creative systems and military ability during a period of extraordinary international struggle in eighteenth century South India. The assessment of Tipu King's tactical procedures and advancements gives experiences into his strategic splendor and the manners by which he tried to oppose the provincial powers, fundamentally addressed by the English East India Organization.

1. **Strategic Adaptability and Hit and run combat:**

   Tipu Ruler's tactical procedures were portrayed by a surprising adaptability that permitted him to adjust to different front line conditions. One of his champion commitments was the successful utilization of hit and run combat, a takeoff from customary European military strategies. Perceiving the constraints of drawing in the thoroughly prepared and trained English powers head-on, Tipu King utilized the moving territory of Mysore for his potential benefit.

   Hit and run combat included quick in and out strategies, ambushes, and shock assaults, making it challenging for the English to anticipate and counter his developments. The thick woodlands and uneven territories of Mysore gave the best scenery to this flighty system. Tipu King's capable utilization of close quarters combat caused huge setbacks for the English as well as made a consistent condition of vulnerability, disturbing their tactical missions.

2. **Mysorean Rockets and Mechanical Advancement:**

   Among Tipu Ruler's most getting through heritages in military advancement was the turn of events and organization of Mysorean rockets. These rockets, otherwise called "congrieve rockets," addressed a progressive headway in big guns during the late eighteenth 100 years. Tipu Ruler perceived the essential capability of these rockets and effectively advanced their creation in Mysore.

   The Mysorean rockets were described by their long reach, exactness, and unstable effect. They assumed a crucial part in different fights against the English, presenting a degree of mechanical refinement that outperformed the contemporary European gunnery. Tipu Ruler's obligation to mechanical development displayed his essential vision as well as exhibited an early comprehension of the meaning of capability on the front line.

3. **Emblematic Fighting and Mental Strategies:**

   Tipu Ruler grasped the mental components of fighting, utilizing emblematic systems to support the confidence of his soldiers and strike dread into the hearts of his foes. The title "Tiger of Mysore" and the related symbolism of tigers were vital parts of Tipu Ruler's representative fighting. The tiger, an image of solidarity and courage, turned into a meaningful portrayal of the

Mysorean obstruction against frontier powers.

Banners, flags, and military formal attire embellished with tiger themes made an unmistakable visual character for Tipu Ruler's powers. This emblematic fighting significantly affected the brain research of the two his own soldiers and the English powers. The symbolism of the tiger, joined with Tipu Ruler's charming initiative, ingrained a deep satisfaction, solidarity, and assurance among Mysorean fighters.

4. **Cautious Strongholds and Key Engineering:**

Tipu Ruler's tactical techniques were not bound to hostile strategies alone; he likewise put resources into protective strongholds to shield key domains. Seringapatam, his capital, remains as a demonstration of his obligation to key design. The island city on the Cauvery Stream was surrounded by considerable walls, strongholds, and defenses, making an imposing fortification.

The development of such cautious designs was not simply a reaction to outer dangers but rather likewise a proactive measure to dissuade possible intruders. Tipu Ruler's emphasis on guarded fortresses exhibited a nuanced comprehension of the international objectives of the time. His essential methodology incorporated both hostile and cautious contemplations, mirroring a thorough military mentality.

5. **Political Moves and Alliance Building:**

Tipu Ruler's tactical procedures stretched out past the front line to the political field, where he participated in complex moves to assemble alliances against the English East India Organization. The Deal of Gajendragad in 1787 exemplified his political endeavors, formalizing a union with the Marathas and the Nizam. These conciliatory drives were pointed toward making an impressive alliance that could challenge English authority in the district.

While conciliatory collusions were not generally stable because of the liquid idea of eighteenth century Indian governmental issues, Tipu Ruler's endeavors exhibited an essential comprehension of the significance of provincial collaboration. These strategic moves looked to upset the English story of uncontested predominance and added to the more extensive setting of hostile to provincial obstruction.

6. **Maritime Fighting and the Mysorean Naval force:**

Perceiving the essential meaning of maritime power, Tipu King tried to challenge English predominance along the western shore of India by fostering the Mysorean Naval force. His endeavors to construct an impressive maritime power were essential for a far reaching way to deal with counter English impact in both sea and beach front districts. The Mysorean Naval force, outfitted with cutting edge warships, took part in oceanic struggles against the English. Albeit the maritime undertakings confronted difficulties and were eventually incapable to break English maritime incomparability, Tipu King's introduction to maritime fighting mirrored his essential vision. The endeavor to construct a maritime power showed a comprehension of the significance of controlling key oceanic courses and seaside regions as a component of a more extensive military procedure.

7. **Assembly of Assets and Military Economy:**

Tipu King's tactical methodologies were intently attached to his capacity to successfully assemble assets. His endeavors stretched out past the front line to incorporate financial arrangements that upheld military missions. Tipu King carried out measures to guarantee a consistent progression of assets for the military, including state command over specific products, the inconvenience of syndications, and financial guidelines.

The assembly of assets was not restricted to monetary approaches alone. Tipu King's regulatory developments, including the presentation of a land income framework in light of direct evaluation, added to a more productive use of assets for military purposes. This military-financial nexus highlighted the interconnectedness of Tipu King's techniques on both the monetary and military fronts.

8. **Appraisal of Effect and Discussions:**

The appraisal of Tipu King's tactical systems and advancements is set apart by authentic discussions and contentions. While many commend his resourcefulness and flexibility in opposing provincial powers, others examine specific parts of his standard, including the treatment of non-Muslims and the direct of military missions.

The effect of Tipu Ruler's tactical techniques is obvious in the verifiable stories that depict him as a brave protector against pilgrim hostility. Notwithstanding, varying points of view feature the intricacies of his standard and the assorted encounters of various networks during that period. The discussions encompassing Tipu King's heritage highlight the significance of nuanced verifiable examination and the acknowledgment of numerous points of view.

6.2 Influence on later military leaders and tactics.

Tipu King's effect on later military pioneers and strategies stretches out past his lifetime, molding the systems and principles of ensuing ages in the Indian subcontinent. The Tiger of Mysore's inventive military methodologies, mechanical progressions, and relentless opposition against provincial powers made a permanent imprint on the district's tactical history. The assessment of Tipu King's effect on later military pioneers and strategies uncovers the persevering through tradition of his essential brightness.

1. **Military Developments and Innovative Headways:**

Tipu Ruler's commitments to military advancements, especially in the domain of innovation, resounded through time. The turn of events and organization of Mysorean rockets denoted a critical progression in cannons, impacting the reasoning of later military pioneers. The viability of these rockets in disturbing foe developments and making tumult on the combat zone turned into an example that reverberated with resulting ages.

The Mysorean rockets not just displayed the capability of native military advancements yet in addition roused future pioneers to investigate and integrate creative weaponry into their munititions stockpiles. The mechanical progressions spearheaded by Tipu King laid the foundation for a more extensive comprehension of the essential meaning of military innovation in the developing scene of fighting.

2. **Hit and run combat and Uneven Strategies:**

Tipu Ruler's skilled utilization of hit and run combat and deviated strategies significantly affected resulting military pioneers confronting innovatively prevalent foes. The illustrations gained from his effective work of quick in and out strategies, ambushes, and eccentric fighting techniques turned out to be essential for the tactical tenet for those looking to oppose provincial or further developed powers.

Pioneers facing strong enemies perceived the worth of lopsided strategies in taking advantage of landscape and upsetting regular military techniques. Tipu King's heritage in close quarters combat turned into a wellspring of motivation for later pioneers, empowering them to adjust and develop notwithstanding difficulties, in any event, when confronted with obvious mechanical impediments.

3. **Representative Fighting and Mental Activities:**

The utilization of representative fighting by Tipu King, including the notable symbolism of the tiger, reverberated in the domain of mental tasks. Later military pioneers perceived the mental effect of utilizing images and symbols to move and spur troops while imparting dread in the adversary. The significance of developing an unmistakable visual character for military powers turned into an essential thought.

The Tiger of Mysore's capacity to make a strong story through representative fighting impacted resulting pioneers in molding the ethos of obstruction and imparting a feeling of solidarity among their soldiers. The fuse of representative components into military missions mirrored a comprehension of the mental elements of fighting that persevered past Tipu Ruler's time.

4. **Guarded Fortresses and Military Engineering:**

Tipu Ruler's accentuation on protective fortresses, exemplified by the essential engineering of Seringapatam, left an enduring heritage in the space of military design. The development of posts, strongholds, and bulwarks for protective purposes turned into a vital thought for pioneers shielding their regions against outer dangers. The significance of key cautious edges was highlighted by Tipu Ruler's fruitful use of protective designs during the

Somewhat English Mysore Wars.

Later military pioneers, confronting the possibility of attack or occupation, drew motivation from Tipu King's way to deal with strongholds. The essential worth of all around sustained positions and the mix of protective designs into more extensive military plans became necessary parts of resulting military principles.

5. **Tact and Alliance Building:**

Tipu King's strategic endeavors to construct coalitions against the English East India Organization affected later military pioneers wrestling with the intricacies of international elements. The significance of fashioning vital coalitions with provincial powers for the purpose of countering a prevailing enemy turned into an important illustration drawn from Tipu King's political moves.

Pioneers exploring many-sided political scenes perceived the requirement for alliance working to make a unified front against normal dangers. Tipu King's endeavors to frame partnerships showed the expected effect of conciliatory drives in molding the tactical overall influence, rousing later pioneers to investigate comparable roads for territorial collaboration.

6. **Maritime Fighting and Oceanic Methodologies:**

Tipu Ruler's introduction to maritime fighting and endeavors to challenge English maritime strength had suggestions for ensuing pioneers confronting oceanic dangers. The foundation of the Mysorean Naval force and the endeavor to construct areas of strength for a power mirrored a comprehension of the essential significance of controlling waterfront locales. Pioneers facing maritime powers drew experiences from Tipu Ruler's undertakings in planning their own sea procedures.

The Tiger of Mysore's heritage in maritime fighting underscored the requirement for an extensive military methodology that thought about both land and ocean. Later pioneers perceived the meaning of sea abilities in getting beach front domains and disturbing adversary maritime activities, repeating Tipu King's vision in this part of military procedure.

7. **Assembly of Assets and Military Economy:**

Tipu King's emphasis on the activation of assets for military purposes, through financial arrangements and managerial developments, impacted resulting pioneers wrestling with the difficulties of supporting military missions. The incorporation of financial contemplations into military arranging turned into an example got from Tipu Ruler's endeavors to guarantee a consistent progression of assets for his military.

Later military pioneers recognized the significance of proficient asset preparation and the foundation of reasonable military economies. The joining of monetary strategies into more extensive military procedures turned into an essential goal, mirroring the getting through effect of Tipu King's methodology on ensuing military principles.

8. **Tradition of Opposition and Freedom:**

Maybe the most significant impact of Tipu Ruler on later military pioneers lay in his tradition of opposition and the intense quest for autonomy. The Tiger of Mysore turned into an image of disobedience against pilgrim powers, moving resulting ages of pioneers participated in enemy of frontier battles. The ethos of obstruction and the faithful obligation to sway characterized Tipu Ruler's heritage and reverberated with later pioneers battling against supreme powers.

The memory of Tipu King as a bold safeguard against unfamiliar hostility turned into a wellspring of motivation during the Indian freedom development in the twentieth hundred years. Pioneers, for example, Mahatma Gandhi and Jawaharlal Nehru recognized the pretended by verifiable figures like Tipu King in developing a feeling of obstruction and the mission for self-assurance.

9. **Authentic Points of view and Contentions:**

The appraisal of Tipu King's impact on later military pioneers is dependent upon verifiable viewpoints and contentions. While many praise his commitments to military technique and the ethos of opposition, others investigate specific parts of his standard, including strict strategies and the direct of military missions. The discussions encompassing Tipu Ruler's inheritance highlight the intricacies of authentic stories and the assorted encounters of various networks during that period.

6.3 Comparisons with other historical military figures.

Examinations between Tipu Ruler and other verifiable military figures offer a nuanced comprehension of his commitments, systems, and heritage inside the more extensive setting of worldwide military history. Looking at these examinations gives bits of knowledge into the particular parts of Tipu Ruler's tactical initiative and the equals that can be drawn with other outstanding commandants.

1. **Napoleon Bonaparte:**

One of the most captivating examinations is frequently drawn between Tipu Ruler and Napoleon Bonaparte, both known for their imaginative military techniques and opposition against predominant royal powers. While their geological circles varied — Tipu King in South India and Napoleon in Europe — their way to deal with fighting shared specific likenesses.

The two chiefs exhibited a sharp comprehension of lopsided strategies, utilizing the landscape for their potential benefit. Napoleon's missions in Europe and Tipu King's hit and run combat in the difficult scenes of Mysore exhibited a dominance of unpredictable military methodologies. Furthermore, the two chiefs perceived the significance of mechanical advancements in fighting, with Napoleon's accentuation on ordnance and Tipu King's improvement of Mysorean rockets.

Notwithstanding, key contrasts exist, quite in the extent of their aspirations and the international intricacies they confronted. Napoleon pointed toward building an European realm, while Tipu Ruler's emphasis was on opposing frontier powers in a territorial setting. In any case, the correlations feature the general subjects of flexibility and vital development despite considerable enemies.

2. **George Washington:**

Examinations can likewise be drawn between Tipu Ruler and George Washington, especially in their jobs as military pioneers battling for the freedom of their particular locales. Both confronted strong pilgrim powers — Tipu King against the English East India Organization and Washington against the English Crown — and became images of opposition and public character.

Like Washington, Tipu King developed an unmistakable visual character for his powers, utilizing representative fighting with the notorious symbolism of the tiger. The two chiefs perceived the significance of mental tasks in getting everyone excited and moving a feeling of solidarity among their supporters.

Nonetheless, contrasts arise in their ways to deal with discretion. Washington, known for his essential partnerships and discretionary artfulness, diverges from Tipu Ruler's unions in the Indian setting, which were many times less steady. Regardless of these distinctions, the examinations feature the common difficulties looked by pioneers taking a stab at freedom against considerable pilgrim powers.

3. **Shaka Zulu:**

A near examination with Shaka Zulu, the tactical pioneer and organizer behind the Zulu Realm in Southern Africa, offers bits of knowledge into the assorted military techniques utilized in various districts of the world. Shaka Zulu, known for his developments in military association and strategies, shares specific equals with Tipu Ruler.

The two chiefs carried out critical changes in their separate militaries. Shaka Zulu upset the Zulu military design, presenting trained developments and inventive weapons. Essentially, Tipu King's tactical advancements, including the improvement of Mysorean rockets and hierarchical changes, exhibited a pledge to modernizing his powers.

Notwithstanding, logical contrasts emerge because of the unmistakable geological and social settings of their missions. Shaka Zulu's strategies were custom fitted to the open scenes of Southern Africa, while Tipu King's hit and run combat and cautious fortresses were formed by the thick backwoods and slopes of South India. Regardless of these differentiations, the examinations highlight the general standards of military initiative and transformation to neighborhood conditions.

4. **Hernán Cortés:**

A differentiating examination can be made with Hernán Cortés, the Spanish conqueror known for his success of the Aztec Realm in the mid sixteenth 100 years. While Cortés and Tipu Ruler worked in various verifiable periods and social settings, analyzing their tactical techniques features the dissimilar results of their missions.

Cortés, driving an immensely dwarfed force, depended on essential partnerships with nearby native gatherings, discretionary moving, and mental strategies to accomplish his targets. Conversely, Tipu Ruler's partnerships, especially with the Marathas and the Nizam, were portrayed by a level of shakiness. The strategic difficulties looked by the two chiefs mirror the intricacies of producing and keeping up with collusions in different international scenes.

Besides, the inspirations driving their missions varied fundamentally. Cortés looked for regional development and riches, driven by the Spanish supreme plan, while Tipu King's obstruction was energized by a craving to safeguard the power of Mysore against frontier infringement.

5. **Tariq ibn Ziyad:**

A verifiable figure from an alternate locale and period, Tariq ibn Ziyad, the Muslim leader who assumed a crucial part in the Islamic triumph of the Iberian Landmass in 711 Promotion, offers a fascinating mark of examination. Tariq ibn Ziyad, similar to Tipu King, confronted strong foes and utilized imaginative military techniques.

The two leaders perceived the meaning of flexibility in fighting. Tariq ibn Ziyad, confronting assorted landscape in the Iberian Promontory, exhibited key adaptability in adjusting to various front line conditions. Likewise, Tipu Ruler's utilization of hit and run combat in the shifted scenes of Mysore displayed a strategic sharpness attached in adjusting to neighborhood geology.

Moreover, the strict components of their missions give one more layer of examination. Tariq ibn Ziyad's triumph had strict ramifications, as it added to the spread of Islam in the Iberian Promontory. Tipu King's standard, while set apart by strict strategies and a pledge to Islam, was likewise portrayed by a more extensive opposition against pioneer powers.

6. **Subutai:**

Drawing a lined up with Subutai, the Mongol general and military specialist during the Genghis Khan time, considers an assessment of vital brightness and versatility across various societies and verifiable periods. Subutai, eminent for his job in various fruitful missions across Asia and Europe, imparted specific characteristics to Tipu Ruler.

The two chiefs exhibited a dominance of flighty strategies and a capacity to take advantage of foe shortcomings. Subutai's utilization of mental strategies, as faked withdraws, finds reverberations in Tipu Ruler's hit and run combat techniques, making a consistent condition of vulnerability for their enemies. Also, the two chiefs perceived the significance of portability in military missions.

Be that as it may, the social and mechanical settings of their missions varied altogether. Subutai's missions were essential for the migrant Mongol military custom, described by quick and portable cavalry powers. Tipu Ruler, working in a settled agrarian culture, utilized an alternate arrangement of techniques and developments fitted toward the South Indian scene.

Chapter 7

Tipu Sultan and Religion

The convergence of Tipu King and religion is a complicated and multi-layered part of his verifiable inheritance. Tipu Ruler, otherwise called the Tiger of Mysore, controlled the Realm of Mysore in the late eighteenth 100 years and stays a figure of verifiable importance, especially concerning his strategies and activities connected with religion. The assessment of Tipu Ruler and religion includes an investigation of his own convictions, strict strategies, cooperations with different networks, and the resulting authentic understandings of his way to deal with strict issues.

1. **Individual Strict Convictions:**

   Tipu Ruler was a sincere Muslim, and his own strict convictions assumed a huge part in molding his perspective and activities. As a ruler, he frequently looked for divine direction through petitions and effectively disparaged strict researchers and foundations. His obligation to Islam was reflected in different parts of his life, from his court ceremonies to his public approaches.

   Tipu Ruler's adherence to Islam impacted his own direct as well as the more extensive administration of the realm. His rulership was described by a combination of political power and strict personality, interweaving the standards of Islamic administration with the regulatory undertakings of the state.

2. **Strict Arrangements and Support:**

   Tipu Ruler's rule was set apart by strategies that mirrored his obligation to Islam. He attempted drives to advance Islamic works on, including the development and reclamation of mosques, the foundation of instructive establishments, and the consolation of strict grant. His support stretched out to Islamic scholars, researchers, and writers, encouraging a scholarly climate that added to the engendering of Islamic information.

   While Tipu Ruler's strict strategies were revolved around Islam, he took on a comprehensive methodology by supporting and disparaging numerous strict networks inside his realm. Hindu sanctuaries, for example, got monetary help and awards for support. This comprehensive strategy pointed toward cultivating concordance among different strict gatherings and keeping up with social union.

3. **Relations with Hindu People group:**

Tipu King's communications with Hindu people group have been a subject of verifiable investigation and understanding. While he is lauded for his comprehensive approaches, there are likewise cases that have ignited discussion and debate. Tipu King's help for Hindu sanctuaries, exemplified by his commitments to the Sringeri Sharada Peetham and different altars, is frequently refered to as proof of his strict resistance.

In any case, the contention emerges from specific authentic records that recommend examples of constrained changes and obliteration of sanctuaries during military missions. The stories encompassing these occasions have prompted varying viewpoints, with some stressing the comprehensive parts of Tipu King's standard and others evaluating explicit examples that might have stressed between strict relations.

4. **Christian Relations and Obstruction against the English:**

Tipu King's communications with the Christian people group, especially with regards to the English East India Organization's development, uncover an element of his standard impacted by international and military contemplations. The Old English Mysore Wars saw Tipu King opposing English frontier powers, and during this period, his approaches toward Christians were formed by the apparent coalitions between the English and certain Christian powers.

While a few verifiable records propose that Tipu King treated Christian hostages with mercy, there are likewise reports of cases where Christians confronted oppression. The intricacies of Tipu King's way to deal with various strict networks during a period of international strife highlight the perplexing transaction between religion, governmental issues, and military procedure.

5. **Iconography and Imagery:**

Tipu Ruler's utilization of strict imagery, especially connected with Islam, is clear in his iconography. The tiger, a seal related with his title "Tiger of Mysore," held emblematic importance as a portrayal of solidarity and fearlessness. The utilization of strict images, including the bow moon and Islamic engravings, was coordinated into the formal attire, banners, and other visual portrayals of his standard.

The strict imagery utilized by Tipu Ruler was not restricted to Islam alone. His consideration of Hindu divinities and images in certain settings pointed toward encouraging a feeling of solidarity among different strict networks. The essential utilization of strict iconography reflected Tipu Ruler's consciousness of the representative power that could impact public discernment and unwaveringness.

6. **Strict Regulation and Organization:**

Tipu Ruler's obligation to Islam reached out to the domain of regulation and organization. He carried out measures that lined up with Islamic standards, remembering changes for tax assessment, land income, and the general set of laws. The organization subject to his authority tried to consolidate Islamic statute in administration, mirroring his vision of a state directed by Islamic standards.

The presentation of another money framework with Islamic engravings and the utilization of the Persian language in authoritative records were emblematic articulations of Tipu King's obligation to Islam. These actions, while reflecting strict contemplations, likewise pointed toward uniting state power and personality.

7. **Verifiable Understandings and Debates:**

The verifiable understandings of Tipu King's way to deal with religion have started discussions and discussions. The variety of viewpoints originates from the complicated idea of his standard, where comprehensive approaches existed together with occasions that have been scrutinized as bigoted. The discussions encompassing Tipu King's heritage feature the difficulties of accommodating verifiable subtleties inside the more extensive stories of strict resistance or oppression.

Pundits contend that specific activities, like the supposed constrained transformations and sanctuary obliteration, subvert the story of Tipu King as a strictly lenient ruler. Defenders, then again, stress his comprehensive strategies, support of various strict networks, and the intricacies of exploring a different and strictly pluralistic culture during a period of political commotion.

8. **Inheritance and Remembrance:**

Tipu King's heritage with regards to religion is a subject of remembrance and debate. In current times, he is recalled by some as a brave ruler who opposed pilgrim powers and advanced strict congruity. Dedicatory occasions, writing, and landmarks praise his commitments to the socio-strict texture of South India.

On the other hand, certain areas censure parts of Tipu King's standard, especially those apparent as severe or prejudiced. The discussions encompassing his heritage feature the continuous intricacies of deciphering verifiable figures with regards to strict character, political conditions, and advancing cultural standards.

7.1 Discussion of Tipu Sultan's religious policies.

Tipu King's strict strategies stand at the junction of authentic examination, frequently summoning discusses and differed points of view with respect to their temperament, aim, and effect. As the leader of the Realm of Mysore in the late eighteenth 100 years, Tipu Ruler, otherwise called the Tiger of Mysore, carried out a bunch of strategies that had ramifications for the strict scene of his realm. An intensive conversation of Tipu King's strict strategies includes an investigation of his way to deal with Islam, communications with various strict networks, regulative measures, and the more extensive verifiable setting inside which these strategies were figured out and carried out.

1. **Islamic Administration and Individual Convictions:**

   Tipu King's standard was described by a combination of political power and Islamic standards. As a passionate Muslim, his own convictions fundamentally impacted the administration of the realm. He frequently looked for divine direction through petitions and effectively disparaged strict researchers and establishments. Tipu King's obligation to Islam was not only an ostensible viewpoint but rather saturated different features of his standard, molding his perspective and way to deal with administration.

   The fuse of Islamic standards into the organization of the state appeared in the presentation of strategies that lined up with Islamic statute. The overall set of laws, tax collection changes, and other regulatory measures mirrored a dream of a state directed by Islamic standards. This adherence to Islamic administration denoted an unmistakable element of Tipu King's standard.

2. **Comprehensive Approaches Towards Hindus:**

   One of the remarkable parts of Tipu Ruler's strict strategies was his comprehensive methodology towards Hindu people group inside his realm. Dissimilar to a few verifiable stories that depict him as narrow minded, Tipu King's rule saw huge support stretched out to Hindu sanctuaries and organizations. He added to the Sringeri Sharada Peetham and conceded monetary help to different Hindu altars for upkeep.

   This comprehensive approach was not bound to emblematic motions yet additionally reached out to the managerial domain. Hindus stood firm on footings of importance in Tipu King's organization, adding to a feeling of strict variety inside the state contraption. The comprehensive arrangements pointed toward encouraging congruity among assorted strict networks, reflecting Tipu Ruler's realistic way to deal with administration.

3. **Connections with Christian People group:**

   Tipu King's collaborations with Christian people group were molded by the international and military setting of the time, especially during the Somewhat English Mysore Battles the English East India Organization. Reports propose that Tipu King treated Christian prisoners with a level of tolerance, and there were occurrences where ministers were conceded security. Notwithstanding, the intricacies of his way to deal with Christians are apparent in verifiable records that describe cases of abuse.

   The vagueness in Tipu King's approaches towards Christians mirrors the unpredictable elements of strict contemplations entwined with international and military techniques. The apparent unions between the English and certain

Christian powers during the conflicts affected Tipu King's way to deal with this strict local area.

4. **Regulation and Islamic Changes:**

Tipu King's obligation to Islamic administration found articulation in regulative measures pointed toward adjusting the lawful system to Islamic standards. The presentation of another money framework with Islamic engravings and the utilization of the Persian language in managerial records were emblematic articulations of this responsibility. These actions were not just expected to combine the Islamic character of the state yet in addition to affirm its freedom.

Land income changes, one more huge part of Tipu King's administration, mirrored a mix of monetary strategies with Islamic standards. The accentuation on reasonableness and evenhanded conveyance of assets resounded with Islamic beliefs of civil rights. Tipu King's authoritative drives displayed an endeavor to coordinate Islamic qualities into the legitimate and regulatory designs of the state.

5. **Iconography and Imagery:**

Tipu King's utilization of strict imagery was an essential part of his standard, adding to the visual portrayal of his position. The tiger, a seal related with his title "Tiger of Mysore," represented strength and courage. The incorporation of Islamic images, like the sickle moon and engravings, conveyed an unmistakable relationship with Islam.

The essential utilization of strict iconography was not restricted to Islam alone. Tipu Ruler consolidated Hindu gods and images in specific settings, mirroring a cognizant work to encourage a feeling of solidarity among different strict networks inside his realm. The imagery related with Tipu King's standard added to the production of a particular visual personality that conveyed the two his strict adherence and comprehensive strategies.

6. **Claimed Occurrences of Abuse:**

Notwithstanding the comprehensive parts of Tipu King's approaches, authentic records additionally describe occurrences that have been seen as abusive, particularly during military missions. Claims of constrained transformations and the annihilation of sanctuaries have energized discusses encompassing the strict resistance or narrow mindedness of his standard.

The challenged idea of these authentic accounts highlights the difficulties of accommodating the comprehensive arrangements with cases that have been scrutinized as narrow minded. Some contend that these activities were reactions to explicit military settings and not demonstrative of a more extensive strategy of strict mistreatment. Others fight that such cases feature the intricacies of Tipu King's standard and the difficulties of exploring strict elements in a different society.

7. **Heritage and Contemporary Viewpoints:**

The tradition of Tipu Ruler's strict strategies keeps on being a subject of recognition and debate. In contemporary viewpoints, he is a provincial recollected by some as a ruler powers, advanced strict congruity, and added to the socio-strict texture of South India. Dedicatory occasions, writing, and landmarks commend his commitments to the comprehensive ethos of his realm.

Alternately, certain segments reprimand parts of Tipu King's standard, especially those apparent as harsh or prejudiced. The discussions encompassing his heritage feature the continuous intricacies of deciphering verifiable figures with regards to strict character, political conditions, and advancing cultural standards.

7.2 Interactions with different religious communities.

Tipu King's communications with various strict networks during his standard over the Realm of Mysore in the late eighteenth century were multi-layered and molded by a blend of political, key, and strict contemplations. Looking at his commitment with Hindu, Muslim, and Christian people group gives experiences into the intricacies of strict elements, resilience, and concurrence inside his realm.

1. **Communications with Hindu People group:**

   One of the remarkable highlights of Tipu Ruler's rule was his comprehensive methodology towards Hindu people group. In opposition to the view of strict narrow mindedness frequently connected with leaders of his time, Tipu King effectively belittled Hindu sanctuaries, foundations, and social practices. His commitments to the Sringeri Sharada Peetham, a conspicuous Hindu cloister, exemplified his obligation to supporting Hindu strict focuses.

   Monetary help and awards were reached out to different Hindu hallowed places for upkeep, exhibiting a commonsense methodology that pointed toward cultivating concordance among assorted strict networks inside his realm. The comprehensive strategies were not restricted to representative motions yet additionally reached out to the regulatory domain, where Hindus stood firm on footings of importance, adding to a feeling of strict variety inside the state contraption.

   In spite of these comprehensive strategies, verifiable records likewise describe occasions of contention, especially during military missions. Claims of constrained transformations and sanctuary obliteration have filled discusses encompassing the degree of Tipu King's obligation to strict congruity. The intricacies of exploring between strict relations in a different society during a period of political commotion highlight the difficulties looked by rulers in accommodating contending interests and strict characters.

2. **Relations with Muslim People group:**

   As a faithful Muslim, Tipu King's connections with Muslim people group were supported by a common strict personality. His obligation to Islam affected different parts of administration, from individual convictions to authoritative strategies. The support of strict researchers, development of mosques, and backing for Islamic instructive foundations mirrored his endeavors to reinforce Islamic practices inside his realm.

Tipu King's Islamic strategies were not restricted to representative motions but rather stretched out to official estimates that pointed toward adjusting the lawful system to Islamic standards. The presentation of another money framework with Islamic engravings and the utilization of the Persian language in authoritative records were emblematic articulations of this responsibility.

In any case, the nuanced idea of his standard is clear in the comprehensive methodology that reached out past his own strict local area. In spite of being a Muslim ruler, Tipu King didn't restrict open doors or portrayal exclusively to Muslims in his organization, stressing a more extensive vision of variety and inclusivity that went past strict lines.

3. **Collaborations with Christian People group:**

The collaborations between Tipu Ruler and Christian people group were fundamentally formed by the international and military setting of the time, especially during the Old English Mysore Battles the English East India Organization. Reports propose that Tipu King treated Christian prisoners with a level of mercy, and there were examples where clerics were conceded security. The intricacies of his way to deal with Christians are obvious in authentic records that describe examples of abuse, particularly during seasons of contention. The apparent coalitions between the English and certain Christian powers affected Tipu King's way to deal with this strict local area, presenting a component of political and vital estimation into his commitment with Christians.

The vagueness in Tipu Ruler's approaches towards Christians mirrors the multifaceted elements of strict contemplations entwined with international and military techniques. While a few verifiable records feature occurrences of resistance, others recommend occasions of compulsion or mistreatment, stressing the difficulties of exploring strict relations during a turbulent period.

4. **Imagery and Inclusivity:**

Tipu Ruler's utilization of imagery assumed an essential part in encouraging a feeling of inclusivity and solidarity among various strict networks inside his realm. The tiger, a token related with his title "Tiger of Mysore," represented strength and fearlessness. The incorporation of Islamic images, like the bow moon and engravings, conveyed a reasonable relationship with Islam.

Critically, Tipu Ruler likewise consolidated Hindu divinities and images in specific settings, mirroring a cognizant work to cultivate a feeling of solidarity among different strict networks. The essential utilization of strict iconography added to the production of an unmistakable visual personality that conveyed the two his strict adherence and comprehensive strategies.

5. **Difficulties and Debates:**

The difficulties looked by Tipu King in exploring between strict relations were intensified by the violent political scene of his time. Military missions, international competitions, and the exigencies of war frequently stressed the fragile equilibrium he looked to keep up with between various strict networks.

Claims of constrained transformations and sanctuary obliteration during specific military missions have powered discussions encompassing Tipu Ruler's inheritance. These occasions, whether saw as safeguarding efforts or as indications of strict narrow mindedness, highlight the intricacies and inconsistencies intrinsic in the ruler's endeavors to explore the different strict scene of his realm.

6. **Inheritance and Current Viewpoints:**

Tipu King's communications with various strict networks have left an enduring heritage that is recollected and deciphered in differed ways. In contemporary viewpoints, he is a pioneer commended by some as a ruler powers, advanced strict concordance, and added to the socio-strict texture of South India. Dedicatory occasions, writing, and landmarks frequently feature his comprehensive strategies and endeavors to make a bound together realm.

Alternately, certain areas condemn parts of Tipu King's standard, especially those apparent as harsh or bigoted. The discussions encompassing his heritage feature the continuous intricacies of deciphering verifiable figures with regards to strict personality, political conditions, and advancing cultural standards.

7. **Intricacies of Strict Resilience:**

The intricacies of Tipu King's way to deal with various strict networks highlight the difficulties of strict resistance in a verifiable setting set apart by political disturbance, military contentions, and moving collusions. His endeavors to adjust different strict characters inside the structure of a principled and comprehensive administration mirror the mind boggling elements of strict conjunction in an assorted society.

The debates encompassing Tipu Ruler's heritage feature the difficulties of deciphering verifiable figures inside the nuanced settings of their time. The comprehensive strategies exist together with examples that have been censured as bigoted, exhibiting the hardships of exploring strict elements during a time of political and social change.

7.3 Legacy in terms of religious tolerance and coexistence.

The tradition of Tipu Ruler as far as strict resistance and conjunction stays a subject of verifiable understanding and contemporary talk.

As the leader of the Realm of Mysore in the late eighteenth 100 years, Tipu King's strategies and cooperations with various strict networks lastingly affect view of his way to deal with strict variety. The assessment of his heritage with regards to strict resilience and conjunction includes an investigation of authentic occasions, debates, and current viewpoints.

1. **Verifiable Setting:**

   Tipu Ruler's time was set apart by a complex international scene, portrayed by the invasion of European pioneer powers, including the English East India Organization. The Old English Mysore Wars were essential occasions that formed Tipu King's rule, affecting his connections with different strict networks. The difficulties presented by military struggles, moving partnerships, and key contemplations added layers of intricacy to his administration.

   In the midst of these difficulties, Tipu Ruler's strategies towards various strict networks mirrored a nuanced approach. His comprehensive strategies towards Hindus, support of Hindu sanctuaries, and backing for social practices exhibited a guarantee to strict congruity. Likewise, his communications with Christian people group and his endeavors to explore the many-sided strict scene of his realm added to the assorted heritage that keeps on being discussed and deciphered.

2. **Contentions Encompassing Strict Resilience:**

   The tradition of Tipu Ruler is interlaced with debates, especially in regards to strict resistance and claimed cases of strict mistreatment. The discussions rotate around verifiable records of constrained changes, sanctuary obliteration during military missions, and occurrences where the ruler's strategies have been scrutinized as narrow minded.

   The contentions highlight the difficulties of deciphering authentic figures inside the nuanced settings of their time. Some contend that the supposed examples of strict oppression ought to be perceived in the particular setting of military missions and vital contemplations as opposed to demonstrative of a more extensive strategy. Others, in any case, battle that these activities challenge the story of Tipu King as a strictly lenient ruler.

3. **Comprehensive Approaches Towards Hindus:**

   One part of Tipu King's heritage that is much of the time featured in conversations of strict resilience is his comprehensive methodology towards Hindus. Monetary commitments to Hindu sanctuaries, including the Sringeri Sharada Peetham, epitomize his obligation to supporting Hindu strict organizations. The support of Hindus in his organization further underscored a dream of strict variety inside the state device.

   The comprehensive strategies towards Hindus were commonsense as well as pointed toward cultivating social union in a strictly pluralistic culture. Tipu Ruler's methodology mirrored a comprehension of the significance of strict amicability in keeping up with strength and solidarity inside his realm.

4. **Connections with Muslim People group:**

   As a passionate Muslim, Tipu King's cooperations with Muslim people group were set apart by a common strict character. His support of Islamic organizations, development of mosques, and backing for strict researchers displayed his obligation to reinforcing Islamic practices inside his realm.

Notwithstanding, the comprehensive idea of his standard stretched out past his own strict local area. Tipu Ruler's organization highlighted portrayal from different strict foundations, stressing a more extensive vision of variety and inclusivity. This approach tested generalizations of strict selectiveness that were predominant during the period.

5. **Relations with Christian People group:**

Tipu King's collaborations with Christian people group were affected by the international setting of the Old English Mysore Wars. While there are occasions where he treated Christian hostages with mercy and conceded assurance to clerics, the intricacies of his methodology are obvious in authentic records of supposed mistreatment during specific military missions.

The unions between the English and certain Christian powers during the conflicts affected Tipu King's arrangements towards Christians, presenting a component of political and key computation into his commitment with this strict local area. The vagueness in his methodology features the multifaceted elements of strict contemplations during seasons of contention.

6. **Imagery and Visual Character:**

Tipu Ruler's utilization of imagery assumed a critical part in molding his visual character and, likewise, his heritage concerning strict resistance. The tiger, an image related with his title "Tiger of Mysore," represented strength and bravery. The consideration of Islamic images, like the sickle moon and engravings, conveyed an unmistakable relationship with Islam.

Urgently, Tipu King's utilization of strict iconography stretched out past Islam to remember Hindu divinities and images for specific settings. This essential utilization of imagery added to the formation of a visual personality that rose above strict lines, supporting the story of a comprehensive ruler encouraging solidarity among different strict networks.

7. **Heritage and Current Viewpoints:**

The tradition of Tipu Ruler as far as strict resistance and concurrence is dependent upon different present day viewpoints. In contemporary India, Tipu King is recalled by some as a courageous ruler who opposed frontier powers, advanced strict congruity, and added to the social texture of the locale. Memorial occasions, writing, and landmarks commend his comprehensive strategies and endeavors to make a brought together realm.

Alternately, certain areas condemn parts of Tipu King's standard, especially those apparent as harsh or bigoted. The discussions encompassing his heritage feature the continuous intricacies of deciphering verifiable figures with regards to strict character, political conditions, and developing cultural standards.

8. **Illustrations from History:**

The tradition of Tipu Ruler gives illustrations to contemporary social orders wrestling with issues of strict resilience and conjunction. His comprehensive strategies, regardless of the difficulties of his time, highlight the significance of cultivating solidarity in a different society. The intricacies of his standard likewise act as a wake up call of the complexities engaged with exploring strict elements, particularly during times of political disturbance.

The debates encompassing Tipu King's heritage present a chance for nuanced conversations on the difficulties looked by authentic figures and the need to contextualize their activities inside the particular conditions of their time. The tradition of strict resistance credited to Tipu Ruler fills in as an image of the potential for inclusivity even in testing verifiable settings.

Chapter 8

Cultural Contributions

Tipu Ruler, the Tiger of Mysore, left a significant effect on the social scene of the Realm of Mysore during his standard in the late eighteenth hundred years. His social commitments enveloped a wide exhibit of spaces, including workmanship, design, language, and cultural practices. Looking at Tipu King's social heritage gives bits of knowledge into the rich embroidery of his rule, uncovering a ruler who succeeded in military and political circles as well as effectively cultivated social dynamic quality and articulation.

1. **Engineering Tries:**
   Tipu Ruler's rule saw critical building tries that reflected both Islamic feel and his vision for a terrific and particular realm. The Gumbaz Sepulcher, situated in Srirangapatna, remains as a demonstration of his design support. This impressive construction houses the burial places of Tipu Ruler, his dad Hyder Ali, and other relatives. The Gumbaz is portrayed by its enormous vault and complicatedly planned curves, exhibiting a combination of Islamic and Indian building styles.
   Moreover, Tipu King's Late spring Castle in Srirangapatna is famous for its novel plan, consolidating components like wooden support points and galleries with dazzling carvings. The combination of flower designs and Islamic calligraphy in the building components verifies the ruler's obligation to making socially rich and stylishly satisfying designs.

2. **Creative Support:**
   Tipu King's support of artistic expressions reached out to different types of creative articulation. The realm subject to his authority turned into a center point for talented craftsmans and skilled workers. The many-sided craftsmanship of Tipu's court, including the development of materials, metalwork, and luxurious weaponry, represents the prospering imaginative culture during his rule.

Tipu Ruler's own effects, like his blades and articles of clothing, are praised for their craftsmanship and elaborate plans. The blades, specifically, are embellished with engravings in Persian, mirroring the ruler's appreciation for both the utilitarian and creative parts of weaponry.

3. **Multilingual Arrangements:**

Tipu Ruler perceived the significance of language in protecting social character and encouraging correspondence. His organization embraced Persian as the court language, mirroring the social and artistic legacy of Islamic civilization. Persian was utilized for regulatory purposes as well as thrived as a vehicle of articulation for verse, verifiable compositions, and official correspondence. Furthermore, Tipu Ruler was known for his help of the Mysorean rockets, otherwise called "Mysorean rockets." These rockets assumed a urgent part in military procedures during his rule. While the tactical importance is apparent, the turn of events and sending of these rockets likewise feature the innovative and logical headways sustained under Tipu King's standard.

4. **Artistic Commitments:**

Tipu King himself was a benefactor of writing and a productive essayist. He added to the artistic scene through his works in Persian and Urdu. His compositions incorporate letters, announcements, and verse, giving experiences into his scholarly interests and social tendencies.

One outstanding scholarly work credited to Tipu Ruler is the "Fathul Mujahidin," a tactical manual written in Persian. This work, which means "The Triumph of the Mujahidin," reflects Tipu King's essential keenness and his craving to report military strategies for any kind of family down the line.

5. **Advancement of Silk Industry:**

The silk business in the Realm of Mysore experienced critical development under Tipu King's support. Sericulture, the development of silkworms for the creation of silk, got imperial consolation and backing. Tipu Ruler's organization carried out arrangements to help silk creation, adding to the monetary success of the district.

The many-sided Mysore silk sarees, known for their fine surface and energetic tones, acquired unmistakable quality during this period. The thriving silk industry filled in as a monetary resource as well as added to the social personality of the realm through its unmistakable material craftsmanship.

6. **Resistance and Interfaith Social Trade:**

Tipu King's rule was described by a level of strict resistance, which reached out to social practices. The ruler's comprehensive strategies pointed toward encouraging amicability among assorted strict networks inside his realm. The monetary commitments to Hindu sanctuaries, like the Sringeri Sharada Peetham, represent his obligation to supporting the social legacy of various strict networks.

Besides, Tipu Ruler's mix of Hindu divinities and images in specific settings, including his utilization of strict iconography, represented a cognizant work to advance solidarity among different strict gatherings. This interfaith social trade added to a syncretic social personality that rose above strict limits.

7. **Advancement of Exchange and Business:**

Tipu Ruler perceived the financial meaning of exchange and business in cultivating social trade and flourishing. His organization effectively advanced exchange, prompting the development of business sectors and marketplaces inside the realm. The clamoring business exercises added to the social dynamism of Mysore, with dealers and merchants working with the trading of products, thoughts, and social practices.

Moreover, Tipu Ruler's endeavors to lay out discretionary and exchange relations with unfamiliar powers, including France and the Ottoman Realm, mirrored a worldwide viewpoint that impacted the social texture of his realm. The collaborations with assorted societies, both provincial and global, enhanced the social scene and added to the cosmopolitan ethos of the realm.

8. **Heritage and Contemporary Points of view:**

Tipu Ruler's social commitments structure a huge piece of his inheritance, celebrated by some and bantered by others. In contemporary points of view, he is a main guarded his recognized as a ruler realm against outside dangers yet in addition effectively supported social dynamic quality. Dedicatory occasions, social celebrations, and galleries committed to Tipu Ruler feature the persevering through effect of his commitments on the locale's social personality.

On the other hand, certain discussions and discussions encompass Tipu Ruler's heritage, reflecting varying understandings of his social arrangements. The assessment of his commitments welcomes nuanced conversations on the difficulties looked by rulers in exploring social variety, cultivating creative articulation, and protecting legacy during times of political disturbance.

8.1 Exploration of Tipu Sultan's patronage of arts and literature.

Tipu Ruler, the Tiger of Mysore, was an imposing military pioneer as well as a benefactor of expressions and writing. His reign in the late eighteenth century saw a thriving social milieu, with Tipu Ruler effectively supporting and advancing different types of creative articulation and scholarly pursuits. The investigation of Tipu King's support of expressions and writing gives a nuanced comprehension of his social commitments and the liveliness of the scholarly scene during his standard.

1. **Imaginative Support and Craftsmanship:**

Tipu Ruler's court was a center of imaginative exercises, drawing in talented craftsmans and experts from various districts. The ruler's support reached out to different types of craftsmanship, including metalwork, material creation, and resplendent weaponry. The illustrious court turned into a middle for the production of complicatedly planned curios that joined usefulness with creative articulation.

One of the most praised parts of Tipu King's creative support is reflected in his own possessions, especially his swords. Decorated with wonderful craftsmanship, remembering multifaceted carvings and engravings for Persian, these blades feature the combination of useful and stylish components. The craftsmanship of Tipu King's court added to the making of antiques that were utilitarian as well as mirrored the modern creative sensibilities of the time.

2. **Structural Undertakings:**

Tipu King's support reached out to engineering tries, bringing about the development of designs that mixed Islamic and Indian building styles. The Gumbaz Catacomb in Srirangapatna, lodging the burial places of Tipu Ruler, his dad Hyder Ali, and other relatives, remains as a stupendous demonstration of his structural support. The terrific vault, mind boggling curves, and elaborate subtleties exhibit the ruler's obligation to making stylishly satisfying and socially huge designs.

Furthermore, Tipu Ruler's Mid year Castle in Srirangapatna is praised for its one of a kind plan, consolidating wooden support points and galleries with intricate carvings. The building accomplishments under his support filled utilitarian needs as well as added to the visual personality of the realm, mirroring a blend of social impacts.

3. **Multilingual Artistic Commitments:**

Tipu King was a tactical tactician as well as a proficient and achieved essayist. His support stretched out to the domain of writing, with a specific spotlight on Persian and Urdu. Persian, being the court language, thrived under Tipu King's standard, turning into a vehicle for verse, verifiable compositions, and official correspondence.

One of the prominent scholarly works credited to Tipu Ruler is the "Fathul Mujahidin," a Persian military manual that means "The Triumph of the Mujahidin." This work reported military procedures as well as reflected Tipu King's scholarly interests and obligation to protecting information for people in the future.

4. **Mix of Religion and Culture:**

Tipu Ruler's support of expressions and writing was frequently entwined with strict and social components. The ruler's solid Islamic personality impacted the creative and scholarly articulations of his court. Islamic calligraphy, mathematical examples, and images were integrated into different imaginative manifestations, mirroring a combination of strict and social impacts.

The mix of Hindu gods and images in specific settings, for example, Tipu Ruler's utilization of strict iconography, displayed a cognizant work to advance solidarity among different strict networks inside his realm. The syncretic social character cultivated under his support added to a feeling of inclusivity that rose above strict limits.

5. **Support of Scholarly Pursuits:**

Tipu King's support was not restricted to laid out types of workmanship and writing; it additionally stretched out to the consolation of scholarly pursuits. The ruler established a climate that cultivated academic exercises, drawing in savvy people, artists, and scholars to his court. The trading of thoughts and scholarly talk prospered under his support, adding to the scholarly liveliness of the realm.

The social and scholarly environment cultivated by Tipu Ruler's support made a heritage that stretched out past his rule. The court turned into a middle for the development of information, with researchers adding to different fields, including writing, science, and reasoning. This scholarly inheritance reflects Tipu Ruler's obligation to military and political greatness as well as the more extensive headway of information.

6. **Support for the Mysorean Rockets:**

While not customarily thought to be a type of craftsmanship, Tipu King's help for the turn of events and sending of the Mysorean rockets exhibited his support of mechanical and military developments. The Mysorean rockets, otherwise called "Tipu's rockets," assumed a crucial part in military systems during his rule. The improvement of these rockets showed Tipu King's tactical keenness as well as mirrored his help for headways in science and innovation.

The Mysorean rockets turned into an image of mechanical ability and development under Tipu Ruler's support. Their utilization in fighting had an enduring effect, impacting resulting improvements in rocket innovation. This help for mechanical progressions further epitomizes the multi-layered nature of Tipu King's support, stretching out past customary types of workmanship and writing.

7. **Inheritance and Contemporary Points of view:**

Tipu King's support of expressions and writing has passed on an enduring heritage that keeps on being commended and bantered in contemporary times. In present day points of view, he is recalled as a courageous military pioneer as well as a supporter of culture and scholarly pursuits. Memorial occasions, social celebrations, and the safeguarding of antiques related with Tipu Ruler feature the persevering through effect of his support on the locale's social character.

On the other hand, certain contentions and discussions encompass Tipu Ruler's inheritance, reflecting varying understandings of his strategies and activities. The assessment of his support of expressions and writing prompts nuanced conversations on the difficulties looked by rulers in adjusting social articulations, scholarly headways, and military goals during times of political disturbance.

8.2 Architectural and cultural advancements during his reign.

Tipu Ruler's reign in the late eighteenth century denoted a time of critical engineering and social progressions in the Realm of Mysore. The Tiger of Mysore not just separated himself as an impressive military pioneer yet additionally as a benefactor of human expression and a supporter for social articulation. The investigation of the engineering and social progressions during Tipu Ruler's rule gives bits of knowledge into the thriving creative and scholarly milieu that portrayed this extraordinary period.

1. **Design Attempts:**

   One of the most famous compositional accomplishments of Tipu King's reign is the Gumbaz Catacomb in Srirangapatna. This terrific catacomb, lodging the burial chambers of Tipu King, his dad Hyder Ali, and other relatives, remains as a demonstration of the ruler's obligation to making great designs. The Gumbaz is described by its monstrous vault, complicatedly planned curves, and balanced format, displaying a combination of Islamic and Indian compositional styles.

   Moreover, Tipu Ruler's Mid year Royal residence in Srirangapatna is a striking illustration of his building support. The royal residence includes an exceptional plan with luxurious wooden points of support and galleries embellished with complex carvings. The compositional style mirrors a blend of social impacts, joining components of Persian, Indian, and Islamic feel.

   These design tries filled useful needs as well as added to the visual personality of the realm. Tipu Ruler's obligation to making stylishly satisfying designs mirrored a longing to lay out an unmistakable social heritage.

2. **Mix of Islamic and Indian Compositional Styles:**

   Tipu King's compositional commitments were described by a cognizant incorporation of Islamic and Indian design styles. This combination of impacts is apparent in the plan components of designs like the Gumbaz Catacomb and the Mid year Castle. Islamic structural highlights, like vaults, curves, and calligraphy, were consistently mixed with Indian plan components, including perplexing carvings, wooden subtleties, and balanced designs.

   The combination of these compositional styles not just exhibited Tipu Ruler's appreciation for different social impacts yet additionally added to the production of an extraordinary visual language that mirrored the cosmopolitan ethos of his realm.

3. **Imaginative Support and Craftsmanship:**

   Tipu Ruler's support stretched out to different types of imaginative articulation and craftsmanship. The imperial court turned into a middle for gifted craftsmans and skilled workers who succeeded in metalwork, material creation, and weaponry. The ruler's very own effects, like his blades, exemplified the flawless craftsmanship of his court. These swords were enhanced with perplexing carvings and engravings in Persian, displaying the combination of usefulness and creative articulation.

The imaginative support under Tipu King's rule added to the production of ancient rarities that were utilitarian as well as mirrored the modern creative sensibilities of the time. The regal court turned into a center for the production of tastefully satisfying and socially critical items, adding to the thriving imaginative culture of the realm.

4. **Multicultural Impacts:**

The building and social headways during Tipu Ruler's rule were molded by multicultural impacts. The ruler's connections with various societies, including Persian, Indian, and Islamic, added to the blend of different components in imaginative and compositional articulations. This multicultural methodology was not restricted to simple impersonation but rather elaborate a smart incorporation of different impacts to make a particular social character.

The Late spring Royal residence, with its blend of Persian-enlivened curves and Indian wooden carvings, represents this multicultural union. The social progressions under Tipu King's standard mirrored a dynamic and comprehensive methodology that embraced the lavishness of different impacts.

5. **Artistic and Social Trade:**

Notwithstanding building accomplishments, Tipu Ruler worked with a scholarly and social trade inside his realm. The court turned into a middle for scholarly pursuits, drawing in writers, researchers, and masterminds. The ruler's help for the Persian language, which turned into the court language, supported artistic articulations in verse, verifiable compositions, and official correspondence.

The abstract and social trade reached out past the court to incorporate communications with researchers from various locales and foundations. This trade of thoughts and scholarly talk added to the lively social milieu of the realm, cultivating an environment of imagination and development.

6. **Military Engineering:**

While Tipu Ruler's rule is frequently commended for its great landmarks and castles, military engineering likewise assumed a urgent part in the social scene of the realm. The ruler's essential sharpness was reflected in the development and stronghold of military designs. Srirangapatna, the island fort and the accepted capital of the realm, saw critical strongholds under Tipu King's standard.

The engineering progressions in military designs were focused on protection as well as filled emblematic and vital needs. The strongholds exhibited the ruler's obligation to shielding his realm against outer dangers, adding to the social story of versatility and boldness.

7. **Combination of Religion and Culture:**

   Tipu Ruler's structural and social progressions were frequently interlaced with strict and social components. The coordination of Islamic calligraphy, mathematical examples, and images in engineering plans mirrored the ruler's solid Islamic personality. Simultaneously, Tipu Ruler's cognizant endeavors to integrate Hindu divinities and images, including the utilization of strict iconography, displayed a pledge to advancing solidarity among different strict networks inside his realm.

   The syncretic social character cultivated under Tipu King's rule added to a feeling of inclusivity that rose above strict limits. The building and social progressions turned into a visual portrayal of the ruler's endeavors to make an agreeable society that embraced variety.

8. **Inheritance and Contemporary Points of view:**

The tradition of Tipu Ruler's structural and social headways keeps on being commended and bantered in contemporary times. His commitments to the visual and social character of the Realm of Mysore are recalled through memorial occasions, social celebrations, and the safeguarding of verifiable designs related with his rule.

Contemporary points of view on Tipu Ruler's inheritance mirror a nuanced comprehension of his job as both a tactical pioneer and a benefactor of human expression. While some praise his engineering accomplishments as images of social wealth and flexibility, others take part in discusses with respect to the intricacies of his standard, including military missions and claimed occasions of strict narrow mindedness.

8.3 Enduring cultural legacy in Mysore and beyond.

Tipu King's getting through social heritage stretches out a long ways past his rule, making a permanent imprint on the city of Mysore as well as impacting more extensive social stories in the locale and then some. The Tiger of Mysore's diverse commitments, including design tries, imaginative support, phonetic arrangements, and military procedures, have formed the social personality of Mysore and keep on resounding in contemporary times.

1. **Engineering Legacy:**

   The engineering legacy left by Tipu King stays a living demonstration of his vision and social sensibilities. Structures like the Gumbaz Catacomb and the Mid year Royal residence in Srirangapatna stand as notable images of his compositional support. These landmarks, described by a combination of Islamic and Indian engineering styles, add to the visual scene of Mysore and act as tokens of the ruler's obligation to making socially critical designs.

   The Gumbaz, with its enormous vault and unpredictable curves, has become not just a tomb for Tipu Ruler and his family yet in addition a social milestone that draws in guests and researchers the same. The Mid year Royal residence, with its special plan and lavish subtleties, mirrors the combination of different social impacts, displaying Tipu King's devotion to making tastefully satisfying and socially rich spaces.

Past Mysore, the design tradition of Tipu Ruler has become piece of the more extensive social legacy of Karnataka and India, causing to notice the multifaceted mix of social components that described his rule.

2. **Imaginative and Craftsmanship Customs:**

   Tipu Ruler's support of human expression and craftsmanship customs lastingly affects the social legacy of Mysore. The talented craftsmans and skilled workers who prospered subject to his authority added to the production of antiques that are esteemed for their creative legitimacy as well as act as social relics exemplifying the ethos of the time.

   Items, for example, Tipu Ruler's unpredictably created swords, embellished with Persian engravings and elaborate carvings, have become social relics that address the complexity and imaginative extravagance of his court. The creative customs encouraged during his rule have impacted resulting ages of craftsmans, adding to the coherence of specific specialty structures in the locale.

   The tradition of craftsmanship under Tipu Ruler's support isn't bound to Mysore yet has more extensive ramifications for the protection and advancement of conventional imaginative practices in the more extensive social scene.

3. **Phonetic Arrangements and Persian Heritage:**

   Tipu Ruler's etymological strategies, especially the advancement of Persian as the court language, have passed on a phonetic heritage that keeps on being felt in Mysore and then some. Persian, known for its rich scholarly and social legacy, thrived as a mechanism for verse, verifiable compositions, and official correspondence during his rule. This semantic custom turned into an essential piece of the social texture of Mysore.

   The persevering through impact of Persian is reflected in different social angles, including writing, calligraphy, and etymological articulations in the locale. The tradition of etymological strategies under Tipu King's standard has added to the safeguarding of Persian as a social and scholarly language, cultivating an association with a more extensive verifiable and social setting.

4. **Social Blend and Multicultural Impacts:**

   Tipu Ruler's rule was portrayed by a cognizant work to incorporate and coordinate different social impacts. The multicultural ethos that penetrated his court, reflected in the structural styles, imaginative articulations, and etymological decisions, significantly affects the social personality of Mysore.

   The city, known for its social energy and various legacy, bears the engraving of this social blend. The combination of Islamic and Indian structural styles, the combination of semantic practices, and the agreeable concurrence of different social components embody Tipu Ruler's vision of a socially comprehensive society.

Past Mysore, this social combination fills in as a model for understanding the extravagance that arises when different social impacts meet up, encouraging a feeling of solidarity in variety.

5. **Military Legacy and Imagery:**

Tipu Ruler's tactical legacy has turned into a persevering through image of obstruction, bravery, and strength. The techniques and advancements utilized by Tipu King notwithstanding pilgrim challenges have transformed him into a motivational figure in the social story of Mysore. The Post of Srirangapatna, observer to extraordinary fights during his rule, remains as a substantial indication of the tactical legacy related with Tipu King.

The imagery of the Tiger, reflected in his title "Tiger of Mysore," has risen above military settings to turn into a symbol of solidarity and boldness. The tiger stripes on Tipu King's pennants and insignias have become notable portrayals of his persevering through inheritance, representing the soul of rebellion against outside powers.

This tactical legacy has added to a social story that praises flexibility and pride, forming the aggregate memory of Mysore and supporting a feeling of personality and solidarity among its occupants.

6. **Legends and Social Accounts:**

Tipu King's heritage has tracked down its direction into legends and social stories, turning into a subject of stories, melodies, and neighborhood customs. The oral customs that encompass his rule add to the social memory of Mysore, depicting Tipu King as a magnetic and brave pioneer.

People melodies and stories frequently feature his tactical endeavors, his support of human expression, and his vision for a socially rich and different society. These social stories serve as a type of verifiable recognition as well as for the purpose of communicating values and standards related with Tipu Ruler to progressive ages.

The consideration of Tipu King in neighborhood fables supports his spot in the social cognizance of Mysore, guaranteeing that his heritage stays a dynamic and developing piece of the district's social story.

7. **Contemporary Recognitions and Discussions:**

In contemporary times, Tipu Ruler's persevering through social heritage is reflected in different recognitions, occasions, and discussions. Memorial occasions, like Tipu Jayanti, commend his commitments to the social and authentic scene of Mysore. These occasions unite individuals from different foundations to ponder the ruler's inheritance and its suggestions for the present.

Nonetheless, Tipu King's inheritance isn't without contention, and discussions encompassing his standard, military missions, and claimed occurrences of strict bigotry keep on molding contemporary accounts. The different points of view on Tipu Ruler's heritage highlight the intricacy of authentic figures and the difficulties of deciphering their activities inside changing cultural standards.

Chapter 9

Remembering the Tiger

Recollecting the Tiger: Tipu King's Persevering through Heritage

The reverberations of history resound through time, and one figure that keeps on instructing consideration and flash assorted points of view is Tipu Ruler, the Tiger of Mysore. Recalling the Tiger involves digging into the complex parts of his life, rule, and getting through heritage. From military ability to social commitments, Tipu King's engraving on the verifiable material is permanent, inciting examination and igniting banters about his importance and the perplexing elements of his time.

1. **The Tactical Maestro:**

   At the core of Tipu King's inheritance is his ability on the combat zone. The Tiger of Mysore procured his moniker through a progression of military missions set apart by essential brightness and relentless opposition against provincial powers. His showdowns with the English East India Organization, all in all known as the Old English Mysore Wars, became characterizing sections in his heritage.

   The unbelievable Attack of Seringapatam in 1799, a climax of the Fourth Somewhat English Mysore War, remains as a demonstration of Tipu King's tactical sharpness. The considerable stronghold of Seringapatam, encompassed by the Cauvery Stream, turned into the stage for a furious fight that would at last seal Tipu King's destiny. The getting through memory of his enduring safeguard against overpowering chances adds to the legendary emanation encompassing the Tiger.

2. **The Compositional Benefactor:**

   Past the front line, Tipu Ruler's inheritance reaches out to the design wonders he abandoned. The Gumbaz Sepulcher in Srirangapatna, where he rests close by his dad Hyder Ali, is a demonstration of his engineering support. The terrific vault and unpredictably planned curves of the Gumbaz mirror a combination of Islamic and Indian building styles, reflecting Tipu Ruler's hug of different social impacts.

The Mid year Castle in Srirangapatna further highlights his building heritage. With its elaborate wooden support points and overhangs decorated with unpredictable carvings, the castle epitomizes the ruler's obligation to making stylishly satisfying designs that rise above simple usefulness. These design ponders act as unmistakable tokens of Tipu Ruler's vision for a socially rich and particular realm.

3. **Social Combination and Multilingualism:**

Tipu King's rule was described by a social combination that pointed toward cultivating solidarity in variety. His help for the Persian language as the court language mirrored a multicultural methodology. Persian, with its rich scholarly custom, thrived under his support, turning into a mode for verse, verifiable works, and official correspondence.

The incorporation of Persian components into the social texture of Mysore addresses Tipu Ruler's obligation to making a cosmopolitan culture. The etymological variety of his court, where Persian coincided with provincial dialects, embodies his comprehensive vision. The persevering through impact of Persian in the social and etymological scene of the area verifies the enduring effect of Tipu Ruler's multicultural approaches.

4. **Financial Approaches and Exchange Drives:**

Tipu King's inheritance stretches out to the monetary domain, where his strategies pointed toward encouraging exchange and trade left an enduring effect. The ruler perceived the significance of monetary thriving in building serious areas of strength for an independent realm. His organization effectively advanced exchange, prompting the development of business sectors and marketplaces inside the realm.

Endeavors to lay out strategic and exchange relations with unfamiliar powers, including France and the Ottoman Realm, exhibited Tipu King's worldwide standpoint. These drives added to monetary flourishing as well as improved the social scene through communications with different societies. The getting through tradition of these monetary approaches is reflected in the exchange networks that continued in the district long after his time.

5. **Strict Resilience and Interfaith Relations:**

In opposition to verifiable stories that frequently portray rulers from the perspective of strict strife, Tipu King's heritage incorporates a story of strict resistance. Regardless of being a dedicated Muslim, he carried out strategies that exhibited a level of inclusivity towards different strict networks inside his realm.

Monetary commitments to Hindu sanctuaries, like the Sringeri Sharada Peetham, highlight his obligation to supporting the social legacy of various strict gatherings. The combination of Hindu divinities and images in specific settings, alongside the utilization of strict iconography, exemplified Tipu Ruler's endeavors to advance solidarity among different strict networks. This tradition of strict resistance has been conjured in contemporary discussions about Tipu King's standard.

6. **The Fantasy and Truth of Tipu King:**

The memory of Tipu King is covered in both fantasy and reality, mirroring the intricacies of his standard. While his protectors celebrate him as a courageous safeguard of his realm against pilgrim powers and a benefactor of culture, his faultfinders feature claimed occurrences of strict narrow mindedness and savage concealment of contradiction.

The mythic depiction of Tipu Ruler as a chivalrous figure, frequently raised to the situation with a political dissident, diverges from verifiable records that present a more nuanced picture. The different stories encompassing Tipu King's inheritance keep on powering discusses, making the demonstration of recalling the Tiger a nuanced practice that requires a basic assessment of verifiable records and viewpoints.

7. **Memorial Practices and Contemporary Discussions:**

The demonstration of recollecting Tipu King isn't bound to scholastic talk; it pervades memorial practices and public memory. Tipu Jayanti, a yearly festival in Karnataka denoting his introduction to the world commemoration, has turned into a point of convergence of both recognition and discussion. The celebration mirrors the different perspectives on his inheritance, with defenders underscoring his commitments to culture and opposition, while rivals scrutinize what they see as a particular and celebrated story.

Contemporary discussions encompassing Tipu Ruler's inheritance stretch out to issues of social character, authentic translation, and the governmental issues of memory. The intricacies intrinsic in recalling a figure like Tipu King, whose standard enveloped both exemplary accomplishments and dubious activities, feature the difficulties of exploring verifiable stories in a cutting edge setting.

8. **Worldwide Viewpoints on Tipu King:**

The tradition of Tipu Ruler rises above local limits, standing out on the worldwide stage. The ruler's cooperations with unfamiliar powers, especially his correspondence with the French during the Mysorean Wars, have drawn interest from antiquarians and researchers around the world. Tipu Ruler's worldwide viewpoint and discretionary drives add to a more extensive comprehension of the international scene of his time.

The effect of Tipu Ruler's tactical systems, particularly the utilization of inventive rocket innovation, has resounded past the Indian subcontinent. The Mysorean rockets, otherwise called "Tipu's rockets," stand out in the investigation of military history and innovation, exhibiting the ruler's effect on the advancement of fighting.

9. **Instructive and Social Foundations:**

The tradition of Tipu Ruler is additionally obvious in the foundation of instructive and social establishments that bear his name. Schools, universities, and galleries devoted to Tipu Ruler act as stores of information about his life and rule. These foundations add to the dispersal of data and viewpoints about the Tiger of Mysore, molding the story for people in the future.

The Tipu Ruler Summer Castle in Bangalore, presently changed over into a gallery, furnishes guests with a brief look into his social support and individual life. Such establishments assume a vital part in safeguarding and deciphering Tipu King's heritage for different crowds.

9.1 Assessment of how Tipu Sultan is remembered in modern times.

The recognition of Tipu King in current times is a nuanced and multi-layered try, mirroring a perplexing transaction of verifiable stories, social characters, and contemporary discussions. The Tiger of Mysore, whose standard traversed the late eighteenth 100 years, keeps on being recalled and deciphered in assorted ways, with his heritage conjuring differentiating opinions, from profound respect for his tactical ability to debate encompassing his approaches and activities.

1. **Dedicatory Practices:**

   In contemporary India, Tipu King is celebrated yearly on his introduction to the world commemoration through Tipu Jayanti. This dedicatory practice, started in Karnataka, means to respect the ruler's commitments to the district's set of experiences and culture.

   Tipu Jayanti includes public occasions, social projects, and conversations that consider the tradition of Tipu King. The recognition has turned into a point of convergence of both recognition and discussion, with disparate perspectives on the propriety and verifiable precision of praising the ruler.

   Allies of Tipu Jayanti contend that it is a method for perceiving his opposition against frontier powers and his support of workmanship and culture. Then again, pundits question the particular account introduced during the celebration, featuring occurrences of strict prejudice and the effect of Tipu Ruler's tactical missions. The yearly festival subsequently turns into a milestone for contending understandings of history and social character.

2. **Territorial Points of view:**

   The recognition of Tipu Ruler fluctuates across various areas of India, mirroring the different verifiable and social settings wherein his inheritance is arranged. In Karnataka, Tipu Ruler is frequently recalled with a feeling of local pride, underscoring his job as a fearless protector against frontier powers. His design commitments, like the Gumbaz Catacomb and the Late spring Royal residence, are commended as images of social lavishness and authentic importance.

Conversely, in a few different districts, especially regions with an alternate verifiable setting or strict sythesis, Tipu Ruler's heritage might be seen with wariness or even analysis. The differing territorial points of view feature the intricacy of deciphering verifiable figures and occasions inside different nearby settings.

3. **Banters on Strict Personality:**

One of the main issues of discussion encompassing Tipu King's recognition is his strict character and the supposed occurrences of strict bigotry during his standard. Pundits highlight verifiable records that propose constrained transformations and obliteration of sanctuaries, while allies contend that such activities ought to be contextualized inside the international and authentic real factors of the time.

The discussion over Tipu Ruler's strict personality isn't restricted to verifiable talk however reaches out to contemporary issues of strict character legislative issues. The ruler's heritage becomes caught in bigger discussions about the portrayal of verifiable figures in a pluralistic and various society.

4. **Authentic Viewpoints:**

History specialists assume a urgent part in forming how Tipu Ruler is recollected. The evaluation of his standard includes a careful assessment of verifiable records, essential sources, and contextualizing occasions inside the more extensive verifiable scene.

The variety of verifiable viewpoints on Tipu King mirrors the intricacies of his standard, with researchers offering varying translations of his tactical methodologies, managerial arrangements, and social commitments.

While certain history specialists stress Tipu Ruler's obstruction against English imperialism and his endeavors to make a multicultural society, others basically inspect occurrences of strict mistreatment and the effect of his expansionist desires. The verifiable evaluation of Tipu King stays a powerful field, developing as new examination and viewpoints arise.

5. **Social Commitments:**

Tipu King's support of expressions and culture is a remarkable part of his inheritance that shapes how he is recalled. The design wonders he abandoned, like the Gumbaz Catacomb and the Late spring Royal residence, add to a positive story that features his stylish sensibilities and social commitments. The multifaceted craftsmanship, combination of compositional styles, and backing for the Persian language are frequently refered to as proof of Tipu Ruler's obligation to cultivating a socially lively realm.

Social commitments additionally stretch out to writing, with Tipu King's own works, for example, the "Fathul Mujahidin," displaying his abstract ability. The protection of Persian as a court language and the support of scholarly pursuits further highlight his inheritance as a benefactor of culture.

6. **Military Inheritance and Imagery:**

   The recognition of Tipu King is indivisible from his tactical heritage and the imagery of his opposition against frontier powers. The Tiger of Mysore is in many cases a battled hailed as a legend against the East India Organization's expansionist desires. The utilization of creative military methodologies, for example, the Mysorean rockets, has added to his picture as a tactical trailblazer.

   Images related with Tipu King, including the tiger stripes on his symbols and standards, have become notable portrayals of his persevering through heritage. The tactical imagery encompassing Tipu King adds to a story of opposition and strength, molding how he is recollected in verifiable records as well as in mainstream society.

7. **Contemporary Political Aspects:**

   The recognition of Tipu Ruler isn't absent any and all contemporary political aspects. The ruler's heritage turns into a site of political contestation, with various ideological groups and philosophical gatherings deciphering his standard in manners that line up with their stories and plans. Tipu Jayanti, for instance, has been a wellspring of political contention, with banters over its importance and the fittingness of praising the ruler.

   The apportionment of authentic figures for contemporary political purposes adds layers of intricacy to the recognition of Tipu Ruler, as political entertainers try to shape public insights in light of their own plans and belief systems.

8. **Public Memory and Social Legacy:**

Tipu King's recognition is implanted in open memory and social legacy, with exhibition halls, landmarks, and instructive organizations committed to safeguarding and deciphering his heritage. The Tipu Ruler Summer Royal residence in Bangalore, changed over into an exhibition hall, furnishes guests with a brief look into his social support and individual life. Such organizations assume a critical part in forming public discernments and adding to the social memory of Tipu Ruler.

Public memory is likewise affected by oral customs, old stories, and neighborhood accounts that add to the aggregate comprehension of Tipu King's standard. The manner in which networks recollect him is frequently entwined with their own verifiable encounters and social affiliations.

9.2 Controversies and debates surrounding his legacy.

Contentions and discussions encompassing Tipu King's inheritance structure a critical part of conversations about this verifiable figure. The Tiger of Mysore, while celebrated for his opposition against pilgrim powers and social commitments, is likewise a subject of dispute, with unique points of view molding the talk around his standard.

1. **Strict Debates:**

   One of the essential debates encompassing Tipu King spins around strict character and claims of strict prejudice during his standard. Verifiable records propose examples of constrained changes and the obliteration of sanctuaries, adding to a story of strict mistreatment. Pundits contend that these activities ought to be censured, seeing Tipu King as a ruler who encroached upon the strict opportunities of his subjects.

   Then again, safeguards of Tipu King fight that his activities ought to be figured out inside the verifiable setting of the time, where clashes between various strict networks were normal. They stress the requirement for a nuanced evaluation, taking into account the international difficulties and power elements that molded Tipu King's choices. The strict debates add layers of intricacy to conversations about his inheritance, addressing issues of resistance, variety, and verifiable relativism.

2. **Memorial Practices and Tipu Jayanti:**

   The yearly festival of Tipu Jayanti in Karnataka has turned into a point of convergence of discussion, mirroring the captivated viewpoints on Tipu Ruler's heritage. While defenders contend that the remembrance is a method for respecting his opposition against frontier powers and commend his commitments to the locale's set of experiences and culture, rivals view it as a particular and politically propelled glorification.

   The discussions encompassing Tipu Jayanti have prompted political pressures, with banters over the suitability of commending a figure whose inheritance is challenged. The memorial rehearses become a landmark for contending stories, uncovering how the recognition of verifiable figures can be ensnared with contemporary political plans.

3. **Verifiable Translations:**

   The understanding of Tipu King's verifiable inheritance is a wellspring of progressing banter among students of history. While some stress his job as a bold safeguard against English imperialism and a benefactor of culture, others basically look at cases of strict mistreatment, constrained transformations, and his expansionist desires. The disparate authentic understandings add to the intricacies of evaluating Tipu King's standard.

   Verifiable discussions likewise reach out to whether or not Tipu Ruler's activities were principally determined by strict inspirations or international contemplations. Understanding the ruler's goals and the more extensive verifiable setting requires a nuanced assessment of different sources and viewpoints, adding to progressing insightful talk.

4. **Financial Strategies and Exchange:**

   Tipu King's monetary strategies and drives have likewise been a subject of discussion. While allies compliment his endeavors to advance exchange and business, lay out strategic binds with unfamiliar powers, and encourage financial success, pundits contend that these arrangements were basically designed for reinforcing the tactical device for expansionist desires.

The financial tradition of Tipu King brings up issues about the inspirations driving his exchange drives and the degree to which monetary contemplations were entwined with his tactical procedures. Evaluating the monetary effect of his standard requires a cautious assessment of verifiable records and a comprehension of the more extensive financial elements of the time.

5. **Local Points of view and Personality Governmental issues:**

The debates encompassing Tipu King's inheritance frequently converge with territorial viewpoints and character legislative issues. In Karnataka, where he is recalled with a feeling of provincial pride, the discussions over Tipu Jayanti and his inheritance become caught with inquiries of social character and verifiable portrayal. The provincial setting impacts how networks see and recall Tipu King, with unique stories reflecting differing verifiable encounters.

Character governmental issues likewise assume a part in molding public impression of Tipu King. The ruler's inheritance turns into an image that different political and social gatherings try to suitable for their own stories and plans. The entrapment of provincial viewpoints and character governmental issues adds layers of intricacy to the debates encompassing his heritage.

6. **Claims of Revisionism:**

Pundits of the festivals and remembrances encompassing Tipu King contend that they frequently include a type of verifiable revisionism, specifically featuring specific parts of his standard while making light of or precluding others. The accentuation on Tipu King as a political dissident and an image of opposition against provincial powers may, as indicated by certain pundits, eclipse basic evaluations of his standard, including occasions of strict oppression.

The claims of revisionism feature the difficulties inborn in celebrating verifiable figures, where the longing to build a positive story might possibly prompt the misrepresentation or mutilation of verifiable real factors.

7. **Contemporary Political Instrumentalization:**

The contentions encompassing Tipu King's inheritance are verifiable as well as contemporary, with political entertainers instrumentalizing his picture for different purposes. Different ideological groups and philosophical gatherings might decipher Tipu Ruler's heritage in manners that line up with their stories and plans.

The ruler's heritage turns into a device in the political scene, impacting discretionary contemplations and public talk. The instrumentalization of authentic figures for contemporary political purposes further confuses the discussions encompassing Tipu Ruler's heritage, as various entertainers look to shape public insights in view of their own philosophical leanings.

8. **Public Memory and Mainstream society:**

Public memory and mainstream society assume a significant part in molding the discussions encompassing Tipu King's heritage. Legends, tunes, and nearby stories add to the aggregate memory of networks, affecting how they recall and see the ruler. Mainstream society portrayals, including writing, movies, and workmanship, likewise add to the development of Tipu Ruler's picture.

The contentions encompassing Tipu King's heritage are not restricted to scholarly or political circles however reach out to the more extensive public talk, where contending accounts and translations are spread through different social mediums.

9.3 Cultural, political, and historical impact on the region.

Tipu King's standard in the late eighteenth century had significant social, political, and verifiable ramifications for the locale of Mysore and then some. His heritage is scratched in the social texture, political elements, and verifiable direction of the region, making a permanent imprint that keeps on molding the personality and accounts of the area.

1. **Social Effect:**

   Tipu King's social effect is clear in different features, from design wonders to phonetic strategies that encouraged a multicultural ethos. The engineering tradition of Tipu King incorporates notorious designs like the Gumbaz Tomb and the Late spring Castle. These landmarks, portrayed by a mix of Islamic and Indian structural styles, stand as demonstration of his vision of a socially rich and particular realm.

   The combination of design components reflects the ruler's tasteful sensibilities as well as his obligation to making a social blend that rose above strict and local limits. The Gumbaz, with its terrific vault and unpredictable curves, and the Late spring Royal residence, enhanced with luxurious carvings, add to the visual scene of Mysore, filling in as tokens of Tipu King's support of human expression.

   Past engineering, Tipu King's social effect reached out to language and writing. His help for the Persian language as the court language mirrored a pledge to etymological variety. Persian, known for its rich scholarly custom, prospered under his support, turning into a mode for verse, verifiable compositions, and official correspondence. The persevering through impact of Persian in the social and semantic scene of the locale addresses Tipu King's job in cultivating a multicultural society.

2. **Political Effect:**

   Tipu King's standard politically affected the locale, set apart by his opposition against English frontier powers and endeavors to attest the sway of Mysore. The Somewhat English Mysore Wars, which unfurled during his rule, were essential in forming the international scene of South India. Tipu King arose as an imposing rival to English expansionism, procuring him the title "Tiger of Mysore."

The tactical systems and developments utilized by Tipu King, including the utilization of cutting edge rocket innovation, exhibited his obligation to guarding Mysore against outer dangers. The Post of Srirangapatna, an essential fortification, turned into the focal point of extraordinary fights during the Old English Mysore Wars, representing the obstruction against frontier powers.

While the result of these conflicts eventually prompted the extension of Mysore by the English East India Organization, Tipu King's heritage as a courageous safeguard against frontier hostility perseveres in political stories. His obstruction is commended as an image of resistance and versatility, impacting the locale's political cognizance.

3. **Verifiable Effect:**

The verifiable effect of Tipu King's standard rises above his tactical endeavors and social commitments, affecting how the district's set of experiences is perceived and deciphered. His reign is a significant section in the more extensive story of Indian history during the late eighteenth hundred years. The Mysorean Battles, with Tipu King at the very front, address a critical episode in the battle against European expansionism.

Students of history proceed to investigate and discuss the intricacies of Tipu King's standard, taking into account both excellent perspectives and dubious activities. The ruler's endeavors to modernize the military, cultivate monetary thriving, and make a multicultural society add to a nuanced comprehension of the verifiable setting.

The Post of Srirangapatna, which saw the climactic Attack of Seringapatam in 1799, fills in as a substantial verifiable milestone. The occasions encompassing the fall of Srirangapatna denoted the conclusion of an important time period and the start of English strength in the area, forming the direction of ensuing verifiable turns of events.

4. **Financial Effect:**

Tipu King's standard left an enduring financial effect on the locale through strategies pointed toward cultivating monetary flourishing and exchange. His organization effectively advanced trade, prompting the development of business sectors and marketplaces inside the realm. Endeavors to lay out political and exchange relations with unfamiliar powers, including France and the Ottoman Realm, exhibited Tipu King's worldwide viewpoint.

The financial drives subject to his authority added to the advancement of exchange organizations and the prospering of monetary exercises. Nonetheless, the addition of Mysore by the English East India Organization brought about changes to the monetary design and landownership designs, with suggestions for the financial elements of the locale.

The financial tradition of Tipu King stays a subject of verifiable request, with researchers looking at the effect of his strategies on exchange, horticulture, and the generally speaking monetary prosperity of the populace during his standard and in the result of the Somewhat English Mysore Wars.

5. **Social Union and Multiculturalism:**

Tipu King's obligation to social union and multiculturalism is a sign of his standard, forming the sociocultural scene of Mysore. The joining of different social impacts, found in the engineering styles, phonetic strategies, and imaginative support, mirrors a cognizant work to make a general public that rose above strict and territorial divisions.

The multicultural ethos of Tipu Ruler's court, where Persian coincided with local dialects, and the advancement of Persian as the court language epitomize his vision of a socially comprehensive realm. This obligation to multiculturalism lastingly affects the district's personality, adding to the social variety that describes Mysore.

The Gumbaz Tomb and the Mid year Royal residence, as exemplifications of social combination, stand as actual indications of Tipu King's vision for an amicable conjunction of various social components. This social heritage perseveres in contemporary conversations about the district's personality and the job of verifiable figures in shaping a multicultural society.

6. **Contemporary Pertinence and Memorial Practices:**

The social, political, and authentic effect of Tipu Ruler stays important in contemporary times, affecting dedicatory practices and public talk. Tipu Jayanti, a yearly festival in Karnataka denoting his introduction to the world commemoration, mirrors the continuous meaning of his heritage. The recognition turns into a stage for pondering Tipu Ruler's commitments, cultivating conversations about verifiable stories, and drawing in with inquiries of social character.

Contemporary discussions encompassing Tipu King's heritage frequently converge with political contemplations, with various gatherings deciphering his standard in manners that line up with their philosophies. The discussions over dedicatory rehearses feature the continuous contestation of verifiable memory and the job of authentic figures in forming contemporary social and political stories.